Inspiring
MIDDLE AND SECONDARY
LEARNERS

To our students:
Thank you for all you have taught us and for being our inspiration.

To our fabulous families:
Thank you for your love and support. Thank you for believing in us.

The authors will be donating a portion of their
proceeds from this book to Challenge Day, a non-profit organization
whose vision is to see that every child lives in a world where they feel
safe, loved and celebrated.

Mission Statement:

Challenge Day provides youth and their communities
with experiential workshops and programs that demonstrate
the possibility of love and connection through the
celebration of diversity, truth and full expression.
www.challengeday.org

Inspiring
MIDDLE AND SECONDARY
LEARNERS

Honoring Differences and Creating Community
Through Differentiating Instructional Practices

KATHLEEN KRYZA ~ S. JOY STEPHENS ~ ALICIA DUNCAN

CORWIN PRESS
A SAGE Publications Company
Thousand Oaks, CA 91320

For information:

Corwin Press
A Sage Publications Company
2455 Teller Road
Thousand Oaks, California 91320
www.corwinpress.com

Sage Publications Ltd.
1 Oliver's Yard
55 City Road
London EC1Y 1SP
United Kingdom

Sage Publications India Pvt. Ltd.
B 1/I 1 Mohan Cooperative Industrial
   Area
Mathura Road, New Delhi 110 044
India

Sage Publications Asia-Pacific Pte. Ltd.
33 Pekin Street #02-01
Far East Square
Singapore 048763

Printed in the United States of America

Library of Congress Cataloging-in-Publication Data

Kryza, Kathleen.
Inspiring middle and secondary learners: Honoring differences and creating community through differentiating instructional practices/ Kathleen Kryza, S. Joy Stephens, Alicia Duncan.
    p. cm.
Includes bibliographical references and index.
ISBN 978-1-4129-4902-6 (cloth: alk. paper)
ISBN 978-1-4129-4903-3 (pbk.: alk. paper)
   1. Differentiated teaching staffs. 2. Middle school education.
3. Education, Secondary. 4. Differentiation (Developmental psychology)
I. Stephens, S. Joy. II. Duncan, Alicia. III. Title.

LB1029.D55K79 2007
373.1102—dc22

                                                                2006101323

This book is printed on acid-free paper.

07   08   09   10   11   12   10   9   8   7   6   5   4   3   2   1

Acquisitions Editor:	Allyson Sharp
Editorial Assistant:	Nadia Kashper
Production Editor:	Denise Santoyo
Copy Editor:	Karen E. Taylor
Typesetter:	C&M Digitals (P) Ltd.
Indexer:	Kathy Paparchontis
Cover Designer:	Michael Dubowe
Graphic Designer:	Lisa Riley

Contents

List of Figures   ix

Foreword   x
    Lance Secretan

Preface   xii

Acknowledgments   xiv

About the Authors   xv

**PART I: INSPIRING MIDDLE AND SECONDARY
LEARNERS**   1

  1. The Inspiring Classroom   3
    Motivation Versus Inspiration   4
    Foundations of the Inspiring Classroom 5
    Honoring Our Role as Teacher   7
    Honoring Our Fellow Teachers   9
    Honoring Our Students   10
    What Is the Inspiring Classroom?   11

  2. The Inspiring Classroom: Theory Into Practice 13
    Three Foundations of an Inspiring Classroom 13
    Five Elements to Differentiate   15

  3. Honoring Individuals, Building Community   19
    Gathering Data About Students   20
    Honoring and Inspiring All Learners   23
    Using the Data to Honor Students   24
    Creating an Environment That Honors Students 25
    Building Community and Honoring Diversity 26
    Using the Data to Build Community and
      Honor Diversity   26
    Creating the Environment to Nurture Community
      and Honor Diversity   28

4. **Creating Lifelong Learners: An Apprenticeship Approach** — **31**
   Maintaining a Balance — 32
   Vital Know-Hows for Student Success — 34
   How to Teach the Vital Know-Hows — 36

PART II: ACTIVITIES AND DESIGNS TO INSPIRE MIDDLE AND SECONDARY LEARNERS — **41**

5. **Lite-n-Lean Learning Activities: Beginning Steps for Inspiring Learners** — **43**
   Investigations for Advanced Learners — 45
   Questions for Discussions and Journaling — 46
   Offering Students Choices — 46
      1. Choices on Homework — 47
      2. Choices on Tests — 48
      3. Choices for Vocabulary — 48
   Graphic Organizers — 50
   Vocabulary Instruction for Different Learning Profiles — 54
   Learning Profile Projects — 57
   Scientific Method Mnemonics — 58
   Adding Fractions Mnemonics — 59
   Interest-Based Projects — 60
   Varying Text Levels — 61
      How to Get Started Collecting Texts of Varying Levels — 62
      How to Use Texts of Varying Levels — 62
   Memory Techniques — 62

6. **Teaching for Meaning** — **65**
   What Is C U KAN? — 65
   Why C U KAN? — 67
      1. C U KAN provides a target for meaningful learning. — 67
      2. C U KAN provides a target for meaningful instruction. — 67
      3. C U KAN provides a target for meaningful assessment. — 68
   How to Write a C U KAN — 68
   C U KAN Sample — 68
      Rubrics for Student Assessment — 68
      Using the Rubric With Students — 73
   C U KAN: Teaching Tips for All Lesson Designs — 73
      Lesson Design — 73
      Management Level — 75
      Assessment Level — 76
      Assessing Group Projects — 76
   How C U KAN Will Help You Differentiate — 77
   Deep and Dynamic Lesson Designs — 77
   Looking Ahead to Deep and Dynamic Designs — 78

7. Deep and Dynamic Design #1: Choice Menus   **80**

Teacher Overview   80

Content Examples   82

Mathematics   82

Science   84

Social Studies   86

English Language Arts   89

Choice Design: Teaching Tips   90

8. Deep and Dynamic Design #2: RAFT Plus   **92**

Teacher Overview   92

Content Examples   94

Mathematics   94

Science   96

Social Studies   97

English Language Arts   99

RAFT Plus: Teaching Tips   101

9. Deep and Dynamic Design #3: Tiered Lessons   **102**

Teacher Overview   102

Content Examples   104

Mathematics   104

Science   108

Social Studies   113

English Language Arts   115

Tiered Lessons: Teaching Tips   118

10. Deep and Dynamic Design #4: Contracts   **120**

Teacher Overview   120

Content Examples   122

Mathematics   122

Science   124

Social Studies   126

English Language Arts   128

Learning Contracts: Teaching Tips   130

11. Deep and Dynamic Design #5: Learning Stations   **132**

Teacher Overview   132

Content Examples   134

Mathematics   134

Science   138

Social Studies   143

English Language Arts   145

Learning Stations: Teaching Tips   148

12. Deep and Dynamic Design #6: Compacting   **150**

Teacher Overview   150

Content Examples   152

       Mathematics   152
       Science   155
       Social Studies   158
       English Language Arts   161
     Compacting: Teaching Tips   164

**PART III: EVALUATING AND COMMITTING
TO THE INSPIRING CLASSROOM**   **165**

  **13. Assessment and Grading in the Inspiring
      Classroom**   **167**
     Ongoing Assessment   169
       Assessment Before Learning   169
       Assessment During Learning   170
       Assessment After Learning   170
     Grading in the Inspiring Classroom: Now They Get It!   170
     Assessing Our Own Growth   175
       Make Time for Reflection   176
       It's Okay Not to Know, But Once You Know,
         It's NOT Okay Not to Grow   176

Opening the Door: Creating an Inspiring Legacy   **177**

Resources   **179**

Bibliography   **246**

Index   **247**

List of Figures

Figure 2.1   Foundations of an Inspiring Classroom   14

Figure 2.2   Five Elements We Can Differentiate (form)   16

Figure 2.3   Five Elements We Can Differentiate (graphic)   18

Figure 3.1   Collecting Data About Students   21

Figure 3.2   Results of a Learning Styles Survey   22

Figure 3.3   Results of a Learning Preference Survey   23

Figure 3.4   Data Index Card   23

Figure 3.5   Grouping for Different Purposes   27

Figure 4.1   A Comparison of Traditional and Differentiated
Teaching   32

Figure 4.2   Stages: Moving Toward Independence   33

Figure 4.3   Inspiring Image: Think Aloud   37

Figure 4.4   Inspiring Image: Explicit Instruction   37

Figure 5.1   Five Elements We Can Differentiate (graphic)   44

Figure 5.2   Questioning for Increasing Challenge   47

Figure 5.3   Examples of Graphic Organizers for Vocabulary   53

Figure 5.4   Two Examples of Graphic Organizers   64

Figure 6.1   C U KAN Components   66

Figure 6.2   C U KAN Sample Learning Targets   69

Figure 6.3   Example of a Clear Learning Target   70

Figure 6.4   Example of a Planning Guide   71

Figure 6.5   Example of Student Handout and Learning Target   72

Figure 6.6   Example of Student Handout   72

Figure 6.7   Example of Rubric   74

Figure 6.8   Deep and Dynamic Designs and the
Benefits of Each   78

Figure 13.1 How to Assess Before Learning   171

Figure 13.2 How to Assess During Learning   172

Figure 13.3 How to Assess After Learning   173

Figure 13.4 Sample Student Grades   174

Foreword

A recent business magazine editorial suggested that "If we hope to fill our innovation pipeline with world-class knowledge workers, then we need to invest in an education system that can produce them. A competitive, knowledge-based economy will require the support of specialists in sales and marketing, HR, law, and general business management." This may be true, but is that all? Don't we deserve more than this from our educational system? Is it not time to aspire to an education system that does more than simply turn out highly trained people who can execute commercial tasks? After loving and being loved, the second greatest human need is to inspire and be inspired. Should this, then, not be the most important goal of education?

For many leaders, running companies, countries, churches, schools, and organizations has been distilled to a mundane pattern of task mastery, leading to a life more akin to the perfection of a Newtonian assembly line. But Newton's theories are history. Life is not made up of discreet, Newtonian, "billiard ball" objects. As we now know, it is a quantum world, consisting of an exquisite interplay between an infinite number of energies. Leadership is about relationships. In particular, it is about inspiring relationships.

My work with the leaders of organizations is often remedial—I find myself working intensely with very intelligent and brilliant leaders who, on the other hand, are sometimes so dysfunctional that they couldn't run the Mad Hatter's tea party, let alone General Motors or France. I so wish I could have worked with these same people earlier in their lives, while they were going to school, for example. Perhaps there I might have helped them to calibrate their life goals differently, thereby enabling them to play out their lives in a more inspiring way that consequently inspired others and made the world better.

Fear has been a prevalent and inappropriately used weapon in teaching for years. "Here is the system. Here is the curriculum. Jump these hurdles in the right order and at the right height, and I will give you a prize." In these teaching settings, fear became the base operating system. Failure to "follow the rules" was failure in a hundred other ways. Motivation manipulates the behavior of others through material, physical, and emotional bribery. It is based on fear (punishment and reward) and ego (this is about me—I want to look good). But it cannot be sustained because, in the end, fear exhausts us.

A teaching friend of mine used a different, inspiring system. He would say to his university class on the first day, "At the end of this semester there will be an exam in which you will be asked a number of questions that will stretch you. My job, between now and then, is to teach you and help you to grow so that you can answer them. I intend this to be a successful partnership." This is teaching that comes about through inspiration, which, in turn, can only come from a loving heart. Inspiration is about serving the other, about loving others so much that, in the phrase of Thomas Aquinas, we will their good. *Stand and Deliver* and Coach Carter rolled into one.

Imagine, too, if we taught students to reflect on why they are here on this planet, what they will stand for, and how they will serve the world with their gifts—what I call Destiny, Cause, and Calling. All great leaders have known the answers to these questions. This is what made them great—and so inspiring. We have the opportunity to make a difference in the world by making a difference in the hearts of students—not just in their minds.

Inspiring Middle and Secondary Learners takes these concepts and brilliantly expands them into concrete methods that help teachers to engage their students, inspire them, involve them, and—what I love best— invite them to be personally accountable for learning. The emphasis is on inspiring and honoring students and inspiring them to learn for the rest of their lives. Who wouldn't be great after passing through an educational system that honors and inspires individual learners?

Ah, now that's the kind of school where I would not have been a holy terror!

—Lance Secretan

Preface

Our decision to collaborate and write this book came from our mutual passion and desire to inspire ALL middle school and secondary students to honor themselves, to honor other learners, and to become lifelong learners. After months, days, and hours of conversations during hikes in the woods, long dinners, morning coffees, and long distance calls, we were compelled to go beyond the talk and take action. We decided to write a book that will show teachers the *big picture* as well as step-by-step instructions for how to nourish the hearts of students within a rich and diverse learning community, open students' minds to the joy of learning, and thus create inspired learners. Diversity extends beyond cultural, linguistic, and academic diversity; understanding diversity shows appreciation for the uniqueness of each individual learner.

We invite you to come join us on this journey. We are still on the path, not at the destination. And to paraphrase Albert Camus, "Sometimes the journey itself is enough to fill one's soul." The new understandings we have developed in the process of writing this book have truly transformed how we view our work as educators. As a result, we are different teachers, we are deeper thinkers, we are different neighbors, stewards, and humans. For us, the journey has become a passion, and we feel compelled to share what we are discovering with you.

As we travel on this journey, we are rethinking the way we teach, the way we view and speak to our students, the way we see our classrooms, and the way we interact with each other. It's more than a rethinking, really; it is a shift in vision and focus. In this era of high-stakes testing, it is a journey that reminds us we are teaching **kids**, not **curriculum**.

What will you encounter as you journey through this book? You will learn about the research and theories that support best methodologies for reaching middle and secondary learners, as well as tried and true, pragmatic, and doable steps for translating theory into practice in your classroom. (Teachers who use the best methodologies for reaching the adolescent learning brain are best preparing their students, not only for tests but also for life!) Using these step-by-step strategies, activities, lessons, and designs will make learning engaging and meaningful for your students while also allowing you to teach and reach your state standards.

But, more important, we believe this journey will allow you to uncover or rediscover yourself. You will recall the beliefs that lead you into teaching, beliefs that may have been buried by years of frustration over a system that requires more and more from us. When you rekindle your beliefs, and give yourself permission to grow and teach using practices that inspire you, you will inspire others in ways yet to be revealed.

So come join us. Remember, it's a journey, not a destination, and the rewards will fill your soul!

Kathleen, Alicia, and Joy

Acknowledgments

As Sir Isaac Newton said, "I have seen further than most only because I have stood on the shoulders of giants." Our thinking for this book is based on the current educational research in metacognitive strategies, learning styles, multiple intelligences, differentiated instruction, constructivist thinking, brain research, and choice theory. We see ourselves as interpreters between the world of philosophy and the reality of the classroom. We would like to thank the great educational thinkers of today from whom we have learned so much about helping students grow as learners. We are indebted to William Glasser, Carol Ann Tomlinson, Patricia Wolfe, Eric Jensen, Lucy Calkins, Nancy Atwell, Howard Gardner, Thomas Armstrong, and Susan Weinbrenner, David Sousa, and The National Research Council (for the wonderful book *How People Learn*).

In addition, Corwin Press gratefully acknowledges the contributions of the following reviewers:

Patti Hendricks, NBCT, English Teacher
Sunset Ridge Middle School, West Jordan, UT

Mansoor Kapasi, Mathematics Coach
Urban Education Partnership, Los Angeles, CA

Kathryn McCormick, NBCT, 7th Grade Math Teacher
Gahanna Middle School East, Gahanna, OH

Sammie Novack, Vice-Principal
Washington Middle School, Bakersfield, CA

Dr. Nancy Reese-Durham, Education Consultant
Department of Public Instruction, Raleigh, NC

About the Authors

Kathleen Kryza consults internationally for her company, Infinite Horizons. She has more than 20 years of experience in motivating and reaching children, educators, and others through her teaching, consulting, coaching, and writing. Her expertise is in working with students in special education, gifted education, alternative education, and multicultural education. She has a master's degree in special education and is an adjunct professor in Special Education at University of Michigan–Dearborn. Kryza is an active volunteer for the Challenge Day programs in Washtenaw County. She resides in Ann Arbor, Michigan, with her partner, Roger, and their "kids" Rennie (the dog) and Sasha (the cat).

Alicia Duncan is a consultant, program coordinator, and teacher trainer for the Waterford School District in Waterford, Michigan. She shares her expertise across the state of Michigan and throughout the nation in reaching and teaching English language learners, gifted students, culturally diverse learners, and inclusion students through differentiated instruction. She has a master's degree in ESL teaching methodology. She resides in Waterford, Michigan, with her husband, Noel, and their gifted (and challenging) feline companions, Henry and Harold.

 **S. Joy Stephens** teaches two beautiful children (on a 24-hour basis!) to honor themselves as unique individuals. She has taught middle and high school students of all levels and abilities in differentiated science, math, and foreign language classrooms. She is a presenter and trainer in practical strategies for differentiating classrooms and inspiring students. She has a master's degree in biology. She resides outside Harrisburg, Pennsylvania, with her husband, Mark, and two inspiring children, Alex and Susie.

PART I

Inspiring Middle and Secondary Learners

1

The Inspiring Classroom

One of the greatest needs of the human spirit is to be inspired and to inspire.

—Lance Secretan

I magine it is the end of your career as a teacher and you are closing the door of your classroom for the last time. You turn the key in the lock and seal a lifetime of work dedicated to students and the pursuit of learning. As you walk down the empty hall for the last time, you can hear echoing voices of past students and what they have to say about you, their teacher.

Will you hear this?

"Oh, I remember Ms. Rennie. Boy could she cover a curriculum!"

"Yeah, she always made it to the end of the book."

"And she sure was funny. Ummm, what class did I have her for?"

"She was the most consistent teacher we ever had. You could count on her to do the same thing *every* day."

Or will you hear this?

"What I remember most is that she taught me *how* to learn. And she taught me *how* to think, not what to think."

"She valued our ideas and our thoughts. She really listened to us."

"Yeah, I loved being in her class. It was our class, not just hers."

What will your legacy be? Will you be known for covering curriculum and rote learning? Or will your students remember you for cultivating curiosity and teaching deep understandings?

Motivation Versus Inspiration

Daily, we face students who are apathetic. They don't engage in learning. They don't ask questions or take on new challenges. We find ourselves continually searching for that "it" factor that will reach our students. In our search, we work harder to motivate them. We offer more "fun" assignments only to have them roll their eyes at us or do the minimum to get by. We try to entice them into engagement with extra credit points and bonus opportunities. Still our students remain unresponsive to our attempts. We ask ourselves, "Why isn't this working?" "Why are my students so unmotivated?"

It seems that much of what we do to motivate our students is similar to taking medicine to relieve the symptoms of a cold. Although cough syrup may offer temporary relief, the cold is still present. We are not curing the cold. Likewise, when we attempt to motivate students with "medicines" such as bonus points and "the fun stuff," we are treating the symptoms of apathy. We are not curing it—not getting to the reasons for the apathy.

Our book came about because of our desire to help educators like ourselves discover a cure for apathy. In our research, we stumbled across the writings of Lance Secretan, a leadership expert and a pioneer in innovative methods for inspiring people and organizations. He is the author of *Inspire: What Great Leaders Do* (2004) and *One: The Art and Practice of Conscious Leadership* (2006). From Lance, we learned that when we attempt to *motivate* another person we are trying to get him or her to do something that is in OUR interest (raise test scores, for example).

> *Knowing WHAT to teach is essential to teaching, but knowing HOW TO TEACH it is what distinguishes good teachers from mere content experts.*
>
> —Gunter, Estes, and Schwab

Motivation attempts to change a person through external forces; it treats the symptoms. (As we already know, motivation is NOT working.) If we truly want to reach our students, what they need from us is INSPIRATION! Inspiration is a stirring of something deep within us all that longs to be fulfilled. It is tapping into the innate curiosity and wonder within all of our students. Only when we inspire our students do they become driven by their internal desire to learn, not by our external "motivating."

If we seek to inspire our students, to find a cure for apathy, we need to learn what makes them tick. We need to ask ourselves, "Why is it that Mark can't learn the information for next week's test but he can easily sing all the words to his favorite songs?" Then we may discover that Mark connects with the messages of the songs; therefore his internal desire helps him recall all the words. If our goal is to inspire, not motivate, we can conclude that what we are trying to teach Mark has little connection to his world. It's not important enough for him to memorize.

If we honor Mark's love of music by offering him the option of creating a song to show his understanding of our lesson objectives, we ignite that internal desire in Mark. Wow! He gets to use his love of music to make sense of the new learning. Bam! The connection is made! Poof! Sparks! Zing! Learning! AHA! THAT'S inspiration!

So with this new awareness about internal desire, our question shifts from "why are my students so unmotivated" to "how can I *inspire* my students?" To be inspiring, *you* must be inspired. In this book, we hope to inspire you by offering you the tips and tools you need to create an inspiring classroom.

Foundations of the Inspiring Classroom

After numerous discussions, reflections, and clarifications we have identified three foundations of an inspiring classroom:

1. Learners who are honored and inspired

2. A community based on honoring diversity

3. Engaging and meaningful lessons

To help us see how the three essential foundations shift our classroom environment from outward (motivation) to inward (inspiration), let's take a step back and look at how these three foundations played a role in classrooms of the past.

For decades, our classrooms consisted of desks neatly arranged in rows. Students were quietly on task, each focused on the same assignment in preparation for the same assessment. In this teacher-controlled environment, there was little collaboration and little place for diversity of thinking or action. Was this an inspiring classroom? Not likely. What was missing?

1. Teachers did not consider how their students learned, and students were not taught to value themselves as learners, so they were not *honored and inspired learners*.

2. Students worked primarily on their own and therefore had little opportunity to honor others for their abilities and contributions. So there was no appreciation for *community*.

3. Lessons were not personalized to students' readiness, interests, or learning profiles, so they were not *engaging and meaningful lessons*.

What followed were classrooms where students were tracked according to their readiness levels.

In an attempt to provide all students with appropriately challenging curriculum, schools grouped pupils according to their perceived abilities, typically based on standardized tests and teacher recommendations. (Often teacher recommendations were influenced by student behavior; therefore well-behaved students were placed in higher tracks while other, less teacher-pleasing students ended up in lower tracks). Once again this was not an inspiring classroom. Why?

> *Never try to teach a pig how to sing. It wastes your time and annoys the pig.*
>
> —Robert Heinlein

1. Instruction tried to match students' readiness, but there was no consideration made for their learning styles and interests, so the students were not *honored and inspired learners*.

2. Students were not encouraged to value all learners for their unique abilities and contributions; therefore it was not a *community*.

3. Since the content was not differentiated to meet students' learning needs, lessons were not *engaging and meaningful lessons*. The result of tracking was that struggling learners still struggled, while advanced learners continued to be underchallenged.

Clearly, these prior attempts moved us in the direction of discovering what our students needed as learners. These past attempts were our best intentions based on what we knew at the time about the learning brain. What is SO exciting about teaching today is that we now have a wealth of research on how the brain learns. This research offers us some very important information about the learning brain as it applies directly to our classroom instruction.

Let's look at how our three foundations connect to what we now know about the learning brain. We know that each of our students' brains takes in and processes information differently, through varied contexts and patterns. We have learned that the brain is a social brain, an emotional brain; it learns most effectively working with others in a safe, supportive environment. Also, we know that the brain learns best when the learning is relevant to the learner (Jensen, 1998). The brain research thus leads us to these three conclusions:

1. If each brain learns differently, then we must *honor* our students by getting to know them as learners and by keeping their needs in mind as we design our lessons. We must *inspire* our students to become individuals who know and value themselves as learners, and who assess their growth as learners.

2. If the brain learns best in a safe, supportive environment, we must create a *community* of learners who respect, value, and learn from the diversity around them.

3. If the brain requires relevance, we must inspire learners by designing *engaging and meaningful lessons* with clear learning targets that connect to their world.

Our students come to us yearning for deeper understanding. In the larger context, the world yearns for citizens who respect diversity, contribute to their communities, and collaborate to solve local and global issues. As the world community changes, so must our classroom community change. It is only by shifting our vision of learning that we can reclaim our students' engagement and inspiration. In this way, we reach them inside our classroom community; they reach out into the world.

Honoring Our Role as Teacher

Why did we go into teaching? Not all of us entered into this profession out of our innate desire to inspire our students to be lifelong learners. Perhaps you were from the generation for which teaching was one of the few options open to women. Perhaps, because of your love of baseball, you thought this a perfect outlet for your passion as a coach and teacher. Maybe this was a career that would be conducive to having a family. Maybe you were born knowing that teaching was your destiny. Maybe you weren't.

> It is the supreme art of the teacher to awaken joy in creative expression and knowledge.
>
> —Albert Einstein

That's okay. Honor yourself; honor your role as a teacher. Then be open to a moment when you realize that you have truly inspired a student. It is in that moment that you can consciously begin to create an inspiring classroom.

For the teacher in the inspiring middle or secondary classroom, there is always an AHA moment:

"I was sitting there with my Language Arts students, under a tree, silent reading on a lovely spring day. Because it was windy, my hair kept blowing into my face, and I kept brushing it away. When I asked a young man in my class to respond to a question, the boy moved his hand across his face just as I had moved my hand across my face. In that simple moment of [his] modeling my gesture, I realized with a jolt, 'This is a very powerful position.'" AHA!

"Mitchell would never do his assignments. In frustration one day, I took him out in the hall, and I asked him, 'What can I do to get you to do this assignment?' Mitchell said he would be willing to draw his assignment. In exasperation, I said, 'Okay!' Well, the next day, he brought in a poster he had drawn. It was beautiful. He was totally capable of processing the information I was teaching. I just wasn't giving him a choice about how to get it out. What he had to offer was never honored." AHA!

"I was 25 and, after four years of subbing, a thankless job that nearly made me leave the profession altogether, I finally had my own classroom. As I stood in front of my class that first day, I looked out at all those beautiful faces, lives that I would touch, and the magnitude of my responsibility in shaping their young lives blew me away. At that moment my job shifted from a profession to a calling." AHA!

These teachers clearly received from their students the inspiration they needed to become teachers who inspire. A teacher in an inspiring classroom has the following core beliefs:

1. *All students can learn.* The preconceptions we have of our students tend to influence our behavior toward them, which in turn can affect our students' achievement. To dispel teachers' lounge rumors of how impossible it is to reach Ben or Susie or Jose, we must enter our classroom each and every day with the firm belief that all students can learn.

Everyone is differently abled.

—Song by Danny Deardorff

Students believe in themselves as learners when our words and actions consistently reflect our belief in them.

2. *All students learn differently.* Inspiring teachers believe that, "Fair is not everybody getting the same thing, fair is everybody getting what they need to be successful." Practical classroom experience makes it obvious to all of us that each student brings his or her own set of interests, abilities, and motivations to learning. So why would we offer only one way to teach them? The key question we must ask ourselves is, "Are my actions and choices providing each student with access to learning?"

3. *Learning occurs through risk taking and mistake making!* No one ever learned anything by playing it safe. It is when something is new and challenging that real learning occurs. If we want our students to be risk takers, we must be risk takers ourselves. Remember the old adage, "monkey see, monkey do?" If our students see us as risk-taking teachers, they will be more willing to leave their own safety zones and take on their own learning risks! And isn't it a good feeling to know that, when we make mistakes as we grow our teaching practice, we are actually inspiring our students to be mistake makers and risk takers themselves?

4. *Students learn what teachers emphasize.* When we look at our students, what characteristics are they displaying in the classroom? Are they disorganized, controlling, apathetic, or impatient? Might they be seeing any of those *same* qualities in us? We must evaluate what we see in our students and then ask ourselves, what do THEY see in us? How can we expect them to be excited about learning, if they can see that we are clearly not excited about teaching? To paraphrase Gandhi, we must be the change we want our students to be. When we LOVE what we do and are enthusiastic about learning, can there be any room for apathy in our students?

5. *Our greatest strengths are our greatest weaknesses.* We all bring special talents to the classroom that need to be used to inspire students. But have we ever considered that our greatest strength could also be our greatest weakness? We may have a great gift for managing a highly efficient classroom. However, this gift may be our greatest weakness when it comes to reaching students who are random, creative thinkers. Perhaps we have amazing energy and a commanding voice in the classroom. Yet, that gift may be an obstacle to connecting with the student who needs quiet processing time. We must continually remind ourselves that we are designing lessons for students who learn just like us, but ALSO for students who learn very differently from us.

In the inspiring classroom, these core beliefs guide our actions and focus our intentions.

Honoring Our Fellow Teachers

There is a tendency in our profession to teach in isolation of others. We come up with our own plans, keep our doors closed, and reflect alone on our practice. Yet, there is tremendous untapped potential to grow our teaching practice when

> *Human beings, who are almost unique in having the ability to learn from the experience of others, are also remarkable for their apparent disinclination to do so.*
>
> —Douglas Adams

we reach out and collaborate with our colleagues. (Two heads REALLY are better than one!)

We honor others, honor their strengths and talents, when we invite them to collaborate with us. If we look around, we will see many opportunities to invite others to join us in this amazing journey. We can . . .

- Honor teaching colleagues. Collaborating with them when writing lessons is a fun and powerful way to meet the needs of all learners creatively. We will design better lessons and have more fun designing them when we work with others.
- Honor learning specialists. Asking building experts within your school for help with learners who have unique needs (e.g., special needs students, gifted students, English language learners) is a great way to brainstorm new strategies for reaching those unique learners.
- Honor outside experts. Honoring the opportunity to learn from experts by attending district and outside workshops presents us with new ideas from outside our schools.
- Honor textbook authors. Many of today's textbooks offer great resources for adapting activities to meet the needs of all learners. Spending some time with that "pile of stuff" that comes with our textbooks, looking for key words such as *adaptation, enrichment, adjustment,* and so on, will give us further resources for reaching students.
- Honor the Internet community. There are many professional Web sites where teachers communicate and share ideas about how to help students. Don't forget to explore the plethora of lesson ideas that can be found online as well!
- Honor parents. Tapping into parents for information about what works at home gives us a bigger picture for understanding the student's needs.

As we honor ourselves as teachers and honor our colleagues, we must not forget one of the most important contributors in the learning experience, our students. Each and every day we have the opportunity to learn something from them.

Honoring Our Students

When we honor our students, it is not just an outward display of appreciation or respect, it is an underlying attitude that says, "I accept you, your spirit, everything about you. You are uniquely you, and I want to know how to reach you."

We honor our students by being joyfully curious about them. We *want* to find out what makes them tick, so we can reach them. Collecting data about our students will help us know them, which will, in turn, enable us to plan lessons that are meaningful and relevant to them. As they come to know themselves as learners, they are better able to grow their skills and confidence.

> If we are to achieve a richer culture, rich in contrasting values, we must recognize the whole gamut of human potentialities, and so weave a less arbitrary social fabric, one in which each diverse gift will find a fitting place.
>
> —Margaret Mead

Each student we have is a gift, given to us for a short time. Maybe they don't always come packaged and filled the way we would like them to be. For a year they are ours, all the same. Are we honoring who they are? Much of Chapter 3 will be devoted to discovering ways to know and honor your students.

What Is the Inspiring Classroom?

We honor ourselves by knowing why we teach, and we use our core beliefs as fuel for our passion. We honor each other by noticing and acknowledging the gifts and talents of those we work with. We honor our students by knowing them and aligning our teaching with that knowledge. When we honor, we inspire. We cannot merely love teaching, that in itself is not inspiration. When the love of teaching comes alive in every interaction, lesson, and activity and is expressed as excitement and wonder for what our students can become, that is inspiration.

The inspiring classroom is not an object. It is not four walls and desks and individuals and tests. The inspiring classroom is about relationships, between us and our students and between the students in the classroom community. The inspiring classroom is an understanding that everyone contributes to the community and, in turn, everyone is nourished by it. These relationships and the community will thrive as each student learns to respect and gain something from the differences that envelope them. A thriving, interacting aura of energy is created—the inspiring classroom community.

There you have it! The power is in your hands! You are a marvel just for the fact that you picked up this book. You desire something different in the classroom, and it's time for a change. With your new shift in thinking, you now understand: It's no longer time to motivate but to inspire.

As you close that door tomorrow, know that you have not yet closed it for the last time. Now stop for a moment and think. What will your legacy be? You have the power . . . to teach, to reach, to honor, and to INSPIRE!!!

2

The Inspiring Classroom

Theory Into Practice

"If I have seen further than most it is by standing on the shoulders of Giants."

—Sir Isaac Newton

When we began to write this book, our conversations focused predominantly on the *practices* we thought would help teachers reach, teach, and inspire their students. But as our conversations evolved, we realized that our *beliefs* about learning had had the most powerful effect in our classrooms; *beliefs* had steered and guided our decisions about our instructional practices. After hours of talking, listening, and thinking, we distilled those beliefs into the three essential foundations of an inspiring classroom: (1) Learners who are honored and inspired, (2) A community based on honoring diversity, and (3) Engaging and meaningful lessons.

Three Foundations of an Inspiring Classroom

These three foundations grew from and are supported by key learning theories that impacted our beliefs and changed our practices. Figure 2.1 captures the connection between our three foundations for creating an inspiring classroom and the key learning theories. As you begin your journey toward creating your own inspiring classroom, know that the effectiveness of these three foundations is supported by a wealth of both research and practice. Our goal throughout the rest of this book is to guide you and provide a toolkit of doable, manageable classroom practices that will inspire your teaching and allow you to inspire your students.

Figure 2.1   Foundations of an Inspiring Classroom

CONNECTS TO:		FOUNDATIONS OF AN INSPIRING CLASSROOM		
		Chapter 3	*Chapter 3*	*Chapter 6*
		Honored and Inspired Learners	**A Community Built Upon Honoring Diversity**	**Engaging and Meaningful Lessons**
KEY EDUCATIONAL THEORIES	**Choice Theory** Glasser	Personal needs are recognized and responded to; relationships are built on a foundation of trust	Focus is on students' building power *within* themselves, on learning *with* students not teaching *at* them	Personal filters influence what we experience and how we understand Mastery learning
	Constructivist	Empowerment; students discover principles themselves; students own the learning	Experiences allow for students to be willing and able to learn; positive classroom experience All ideas are valued	Students create meaning using prior knowledge to construct own understanding
	Brain Research	Each brain takes in and processes information *differently*, through varied contexts and patterns	The brain is a social brain, an emotional brain; it learns most effectively working with others in a safe, supportive community	The brain learns best when the learning is relevant to the learner
HIGH-QUALITY CURRICULUM				

If we reflect upon these foundational theories, it becomes obvious that one-size-fits-all practices don't work. Therefore, if we are to honor and inspire all learners in our classrooms, we need to find engaging and meaningful paths to differentiate our instruction and meet our district learning targets. Think back over your past few weeks of teaching. Ask yourself the following questions:

- Have I set a tone in the room that respects and honors all learners? How do I know? What evidence can I provide that I have honored my students?

- Is the physical environment in my classroom invigorating and student centered?
- Is there a sense of community in my classroom? Do students respect each other? Do they learn and grow together?
- Do I offer various ways for students to access the content I am teaching? What are those ways?
- Do I present new ideas and information to students in various ways?
- How do I allow students to process what I just taught them? Do they have a choice in how they get to process new learning?
- How do I check for understanding? Do I take into consideration that students show understanding in different ways?

> *You may be the ones to learn how to weave these three strengths together: a swirling spiral of our unique gifts, our desire for community, and our need for individual freedom. If you figure this out, we will move forward as a planetary community where people experience what it means to be fully human.*
>
> —Margaret Wheatley

Reflecting on our answers to these questions, we should begin to get a picture of whether our teaching style and our beliefs are in alignment with the three foundations of the inspiring classroom. We should also notice the balance we offer in terms of routine and novelty in our classrooms.

Five Elements to Differentiate

The learning brain requires both novelty and routine (Sousa, 2006). We *must* build routine into our teaching day. The procedures we teach our students (how to enter and exit the classroom, work in groups, turn in papers, etc.) become the routines that allow our classroom to flow smoothly, that create more time for us to teach effectively.

However, if we follow the same *teaching* pattern each day (read the book, do the questions or worksheet, take a quiz or test), chances are students are not going to look at us, eyes shining with wonder and enthusiasm, as they learn our subject. Teaching using repetitive methods does not honor our students' needs to access learning in a variety of ways. Routine teaching is guaranteed to make students lose their passion for learning!

To *nurture* students' passion for learning, there are five elements we can differentiate in our classroom instruction. Figure 2.2 is an overview of those elements.

It is important, in becoming inspiring teachers, that we note which of the elements we are already skilled at, or are working toward developing, and which elements we most need to develop.

An easy framework to begin or extend our skills at honoring all learners is by designing our lessons using the *Chunk*, *Chew*, and *Check* steps.

Figure 2.2   Five Elements We Can Differentiate

Three Steps of Every Lesson			The Fundamentals	
1. Input	**2. Process**	**3. Output**	**The Information**	**Environment**
Information In		*Information Out*		
Taking in new chunks of information through ❑ Seeing the information in charts/graphs/notes ❑ Reading information from books, magazines, online ❑ Hearing the information through lecture/discussions ❑ Manipulating, doing, or building to gain the information	**Making sense of new of information by** ❑ Writing to help them connect the new information ❑ Drawing pictures/concept maps to connect the new information ❑ Talking or listening to connect the new information ❑ Doing, manipulating, or building to connect the new information	**Showing understanding and knowledge of information by** ❑ Selecting from various problems in a text book to show their understanding ❑ Choosing different projects that show their understanding of what they've learned according to their strengths: Write a poem Sing a song Build a project Make a video ❑ Showing what they learn through projects of varying difficulty based on student's readiness	❑ Reading different texts that are easier/harder ❑ Using alternative methods (videos, tapes, experiments, computers) at easier or harder levels ❑ Exploring information through different levels of questioning ❑ Exploring information through varying levels of depth and complexity ❑ Exploring information through personal interests	**Affective Atmosphere** ❑ Students' strengths are acknowledged and used to help them grow and learn ❑ Risk taking and mistake making are encouraged. ❑ The relationships within the learning community are focused on helping one another grow **Physical Setting** ❑ The energy level of the learning environment changes depending on the goal/task; sometimes relaxed focused learning, sometimes enthusiastic investigations ❑ The lighting, seating, temperature, and sounds in the environment change to meet various needs on various days. ❑ The physical location for learning changes according to the outcome/goal ❑ Students work with varied groupings depending on the learning goal. ❑ Student movement and material management supports student independence; they know what to do without asking
Chunk	**Chew**	**Check**		

CHUNK: *new information is presented to the learner.* The brain learns best when it receives new information in small chunks. Because each brain perceives incoming information differently, we need to vary how we offer chunks of new learning.

CHEW: *the learner has to make sense of the information.* Each brain has a unique way of connecting new information to what it already knows. Therefore, we need to offer students a variety of ways to CHEW on new information we have presented to them.

CHECK: *the teacher checks whether the learner has processed the information.* We know that individuals possess unique talents and therefore demonstrate understanding in unique ways. We need to balance the ways we CHECK for student understanding.

Keeping the *Chunk*, *Chew*, and *Check* framework in mind as we design our lessons helps us vary our teaching and offer better access to learning for all students in our classrooms. We also need to support differentiating by creating an environment and working with the content in ways that honor all learners.

ENVIRONMENT: *tone and setting of the classroom.* The learning brain learns best in a safe environment. We need to work to build a community and an environment that respects all learners and offers them safe access to learning.

CONTENT: *what we teach.* Our students come to us with different readiness levels and different interests. We need to teach to the same learning objectives, but vary the content based on the readiness levels or interests of our students.

This overview of the three foundations and five elements of the inspiring classroom gives us a framework, a schema, to guide our thinking. Throughout the rest of this book, we offer concrete and practical strategies for creating the inspiring classroom. Remember, we must be guided *first* by our beliefs. When we teach from our beliefs, the practices will follow.

Figure 2.3   Five Elements We Can Differentiate

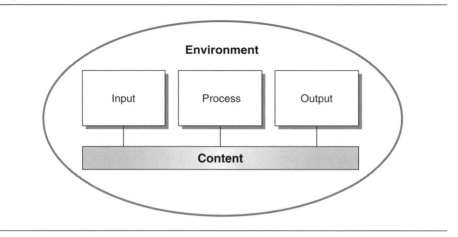

3

Honoring Individuals, Building Community

Without an understanding of the unique meanings existing for the individual, the problems of helping him effectively are almost insurmountable.

—Arthur Combs

As we were working on this book, Joy called and shared this amazing story with us:

She was stealing a few quiet moments in the bathroom while her son, Alex, was outside the door rattling a set of plastic keys. After pretending to search for the bathroom key, he finally burst through the door with a look of pure excitement on his face and announced that he had found *the right key*. "Oh, Alex," Joy exclaimed. "That is such a special key that you have!" Then, in that rare wisdom of children's teaching, he declared, "Mommy, all these keys are special because each door is different, and it takes other special keys to open them."

Like Alex and his keys, the diversity in our classrooms, both academically and culturally, presents us with two options. We can recognize that our students are all different, yet continue with the one-size-fits-all teaching we've always done—using one key to try to open 30 different doors. Or we can recognize and respond to those differences by saying to our students, "The door to how each of you learns is different; please work with me to find the key that will help you to understand and grow as a learner." As diverse and unique as each of our students is, there is a pathway to deeper learning and inspiration to be found within them. When we follow our beliefs, when we opt to open the doors to all students' learning, we find our inspiration for teaching and are, in return, an inspiration to our students.

In an inspiring classroom, the unspoken messages students receive from us are . . .

- "Let's search together for your key. I won't pick your lock, beat down your door, or call a locksmith to change your lock. Your lock and door are unique and valued here." (Honored and inspired learners)
- "Let's share our keys with each other. Imagine how many doors will open and what lies ahead for us when we learn and grow together." (Building community through honoring diversity)
- "Once I find your key, I will do my best to use it to open the doors to the subject I am teaching you. I will find connections between what I teach and how you learn." (Engaging and meaningful lessons)

These are the messages that help us invent a world of possibilities in our classrooms. If this is the world we want to create for our students, then it's time to grab our key rings, open the doors to possibilities, and gather data to help us lay down the first two of the three foundations of the inspiring classroom: *honored and inspired learners* and *building community through honoring diversity*.

Gathering Data About Students

As Combs, an educational psychologist, emphasized in this chapter's opening quotation, we must *know* our students, first and foremost, to understand the many ways they make meaning. The most efficient and effective way to know your students is to gather data about them. (See the "Resources" section for example surveys and inventories.)

Figure 3.1 suggests the types of data you can collect, how to collect information, and examples of how to use the data to help you teach more effectively and efficiently.

Figure 3.1   Collecting Data About Students

Data	What It Is	How to Collect	Use It For
Academic scores	Grades, standardized tests, pretests	Student records, formal and informal observations, test scores	Working with students by readiness levels
Learning preferences	Preferences students have regarding their learning environment	Learning preference surveys, student interviews, journaling prompts, discussions	Changing the physical environment to offer choices for how students work: on the floor, walking around, near a window, soft music playing, etc.
Learning styles	The way in which a student chunks, chews, and checks new information	Multiple intelligences surveys Sternberg's intelligences surveys Learning style surveys	Inform instruction to adapt to varying learning styles, grouping students by similar or varied learning styles, offering assignment choices with specific learning styles in mind
Interest inventories	Noting students' general interests, attitudes they have about subject areas, or content-specific interests	Quick writes, general and content-specific interest surveys, letter to the teacher, classroom discussion	Grouping students with similar interests, prime new learning by making connections to their interests, offering choices based on their interests

As you start to gather data about your students, begin with small steps. Choose one survey that you feel will most benefit you and tell you what you want to know about your students. The earlier in the year you conduct the surveys, the sooner you will know your students and can begin to design lessons that honor their learning differences. Once you conduct the surveys, it is essential to use the data on the surveys. Otherwise, at the end of the year, you will find a pile of surveys in the back of the room that you never used! Here are three examples of how teachers found user-friendly formats for gathering data about their students.

Ms. Jones, a middle school science teacher who is new to teaching, gave her students a *learning styles survey*. She asked them to tell her what they needed in order to succeed in science. Ms. Jones gathered the data by making a *one-page list* with her students' names on it (see

Figure 3.2). In one column she noted each student's top two or three learning styles, and, in the next column, she noted their comments about what they needed to be successful in science.

Figure 3.2   Results of a Learning Styles Survey

Name	Learning Styles	Student Comments
Tyler	Listening, Manipulating	Keep science the same
Melissa	Listening	
Brittany	Speaking, Reading	Challenge her
	Listening, Manipulating	Hands-on
Kyle	Listening, Manipulating	More hands-on
Chelsea	Speaking, Visualizing	
Helena	Visualizing	Challenge her
Frederick	Visualizing	Challenge him
Nicole	Listening	
Emily	Writing, Manipulating	Science is tough, go over test questions
Alexandra	Manipulating	Likes science; doesn't need extra challenges
Anthony	Listening, Visualizing	Has fun in science; more discussions
Jayson	Reading, Manipulating	Doesn't really like science
Matthew	Listening, Manipulating	More hands-on
Yuriy	Listening	Likes science; works well with partners
Megan	Manipulating	Likes science; more hands-on
Ashley	Manipulating	Type vs. write; doesn't like standing in front

Mr. Pothus, a high school math teacher, uses *tick marks* to collect data about the learning preferences of his math students. He compiled the data from each survey onto one survey that he keeps close at hand for reference.

Ms. Smythe, an experienced high school teacher, created a *learning profile system* for better understanding her students by using 4 × 6 index cards. She does several different types of surveys throughout the first month of school. She summarizes her findings onto one card for each student (see Figure 3.4). She comments, "You know, it's sort of a pain to do the surveys and gather the data, but I now know about my students in September what I used to not know about them until April."

Three different teachers, three different points in their professional growth, three different ways to gather data. Yet each of them understands the importance of getting to know their students. Now, let's look at how they use the data to honor their students and build community.

Figure 3.3   Results of a Learning Preference Survey

Totals:

Yes	No		Sometimes
13	6	1. I study best when it is quiet.	1
12	8	2. I am able to ignore the noise of other people talking while I am working.	
13	7	3. I like to work at a table or desk.	
4	14	4. I like to work on the floor.	2
13	5	5. I work hard for myself.	2
11	8	6. I work hard for my parents or teacher.	1
6	13	7. I will work on an assignment until it is completed, no matter what.	1
17	2	8. Sometimes I get frustrated with my work and do not finish it.	1

Figure 3.4   Data Index Card

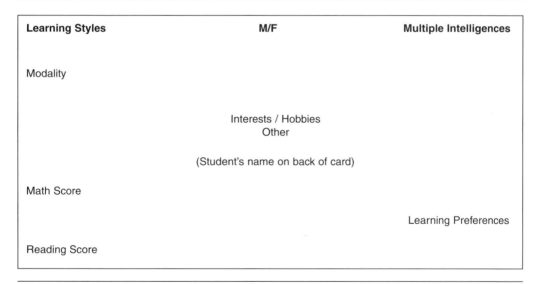

Honoring and Inspiring All Learners

The first of the three foundations of an inspiring classroom is honoring and inspiring all learners. Below, we will look at how we can use the data we have gathered to build this foundation and create a nourishing classroom environment.

Using the Data to Honor Students

When you have the data gathered in one easily accessible format, you can use the data to readily inform your instructional practice and honor individual learners. Let's take a look at how Ms. Jones, Mr. Pothus, and Ms. Smythe use their data.

Ms. Jones noted that several of her students said that they wanted more challenge in science class. Looking at the data, Ms. Jones realized that she could not neglect the advanced learners in her class. She adjusted the depth and complexity of her lessons to provide them more challenge. She is honoring students by responding to the needs of her advanced learners.

Mr. Pothus is surprised to find that 17 out of 19 students in his pre-algebra class quit when they feel frustrated. He realized that, in order to keep them engaged, he must lower the frustration level caused by his assignments and help his students by teaching them strategies for persevering on challenging tasks. Mr. Pothus also noted that four of his students said that they liked working on the floor. Against his better judgment, he allowed them to do so and was surprised to find that these students got their work done much more effectively in this prone position!

> Knowing others is wisdom, knowing yourself is enlightenment.
>
> —Lao Tzu

Mrs. Smythe knows from looking at her learner profile cards that John loves reading in groups and learns most from seeing or creating a mind map. Sally loves to act things out and learns best using movement to help her remember things. Mrs. Smythe frequently thumbs through the data file, either before tests to vary the objective response sections or while planning a unit and offering choices for an assignment. Honoring each learner's differences is what makes these educators teachers who inspire their students to do their best!

We can also use the data we have gathered to help our students know themselves: their strengths, their weaknesses, their processes of learning. When students can identify their strengths as learners, they become empowered and can make appropriate choices when it comes to their learning. Students then begin to *own* that learning. They are clear on what they need as a learner and can advocate for themselves.

Students can advocate for themselves by

- Choosing appropriately challenging activities
- Building their interests into projects they are doing
- When seeking clarity, choosing a partner who processes like themselves

- Reflecting on whether the learning processes they are using are working for them and if not, what might work better

Creating an Environment That Honors Students

We create an environment where students are honored and inspired in three ways: through the physical setting, the routines we establish, and the emotional tone in our classrooms. In creating a *physical environment* that honors all learners, we can . . .

- Change the energy level of the learning environment to meet learning goals (e.g., relaxed reflection vs. exciting investigation).
- Adjust the lighting to suit the learners.
- Provide music for some students to listen to in small groups if that is how they study best.
- Adjust the location in which individuals can work by offering options in the use of classroom space.
- Change *our* location—walk around the room or teach from a different spot in the classroom.

The learning brain needs *routine* and predictability. Our students feel safe when they know how our classrooms function. Once students are comfortable with the routines in the learning environment, they can more readily welcome a challenge or new situation. Students are focused on the task at hand with no thought of "What do I do now?" when we teach them routines such as . . .

- How to enter and exit the room
- Where and when to turn in papers
- How and whom to ask for help
- How to transition from traditional seating arrangements into groups
- Where to go for supplies and materials for activities
- What to do when they are finished with tasks but others are not

We also want to be aware of the *emotional tone* we set in our classrooms. Research shows that first impressions are made up of the following: 55 % visual impact, 38 % tone, and 7 % what you actually say (Association of Graduate Careers Advisory Services, 2005). We want our students to feel welcomed by the learning environment. We want to create a space for our students where they feel safe making mistakes, safe being different, safe knowing they are accepted without condition.

Strategies for creating a positive, affective tone in our classrooms include

• Affirmation posters. Students will know exactly what is important to us when our core beliefs are clearly defined and visible for all to see. Two messages that are essential to post in our classrooms: "This is a risk-taking, mistake-making classroom" and "Fair is not everyone getting the same thing, fair is everyone getting what they need to be successful." When we post these beliefs and live by them, we provide students with a powerful reminder that their needs are honored and that we are in this learning process together, mistakes and all!

Anyone who has never made a mistake has never tried anything new.

—Albert Einstein

• Modeling honor and inspiration. Robert Fulghum once said, "Don't worry that children never listen to you; worry that they are always watching you." Our students look to see if we are walking the walk of the messages we have posted on our walls. Imagine this scenario. Kendra is struggling with understanding geometry. Sensing Kendra's frustration, the teacher provides her with a set of manipulatives to help her understand the concept. Other students see this teacher is living what he believes. It is clear Kendra *is* getting what she needs to succeed, and the rest of the students know the same will be true for them. That's fair!

Students who know and value themselves as learners and feel safe in their learning environment realize that they have an important place in the learning community. Students who honor themselves as learners are more able to respect and honor other learners.

Building Community and Honoring Diversity

We've learned ways to build the first foundation of the inspiring classroom, honoring and inspiring our students as individuals, now we will show you how to build the second foundation, building community through honoring diversity.

Using the Data to Build Community and Honor Diversity

A teacher cannot build a community of learners unless the voices and lives of the students are an integral part of the curriculum.

—Peterson

The brain is a social brain and learns best in a community. In the inspiring classroom, we look at diversity as an opportunity to grow in ways we couldn't otherwise. Looking at the data we gather, we see that diversity is a rich source from which to build community. Here is how our three teachers used data to build their communities.

When Ms. Jones saw from her list (Figure 3.2) that many students in her class learned best by touching and moving, she incorporated more hands-on learning and movement into her lessons to help students remember key information. When his class got too noisy, Mr. Pothus used the survey data to remind his students that the majority of them said they were able to learn better when the class was quiet. The class got quiet!

After looking at the vocabulary for the social studies unit, Ms. Smythe felt that students would understand the vocabulary most effectively if they were placed with students of the same multiple intelligence. Pulling out her data index cards (Figure 3.4) the evening before class, she was able to arrange students quickly into art smart, word smart, body smart, and music smart groups. Students worked with others of the same intelligence strength to draw words, create word clues, do word charades, and compose word songs or rhythms. Students then shared their creations with others. Students who work in community with others of the same learning strength begin to internalize the learning and study skills that work best for them. Ms. Smythe used the cards again to group students for a multimedia research project. She recognized that, this time, the final product would be more creative if students worked with others who had *different* learning styles and strengths.

When teachers in the inspiring classroom use data to help them strategically group learners for different purposes, students begin to see the power in learning with others who learn like them. There are several different types of grouping that can be used in the inspiring classroom.

Figure 3.5   Grouping for Different Purposes

Purpose for Grouping	Group Students By
You are teaching a unit on Europe. Students' surveys show that students are really interested in certain countries.	Interests (this will change based on interest inventories)
It's the beginning of the year and you are starting your unit on adventure, which your students love. You want to see what kind of choices they make about working together.	Choice (students pick or you pick by random draw)
The pretest you gave before the fraction unit showed that some students already know your objectives, some are ready to learn them, and others are struggling with the concept.	Readiness
You want students to remember the steps for the writing process. You want them to create a mnemonic that works for them in remembering the steps.	Same learning style

It's okay to make the reasons for grouping students as clear to your students as they are to you. They can understand that when they are placed in groups of peers with similar readiness, it is because they are at the same point in learning the new content and that they will learn it best from this place. When they are placed in groups of the same learning style, they will be processing a concept with others who think like themselves so that they can study using techniques that work best for them. For a research-based project, students know they may benefit the most when they are placed with students with similar interests (or with different skills). We honor our students when we value their strengths and the areas in which they need to grow. We inspire them when we place them in groups so that their talents benefit the entire community.

Creating the Environment to Nurture Community and Honor Diversity

Previously, we discussed creating an environment that honors and inspires individual students. Now let's look at how to create an environment that nurtures a thriving and diverse community. Again, we'll look at the physical setting, the classroom routines, and the environmental tone.

1. In creating a *physical environment* that builds community, you can . . .
   - Create places for groups to work
   - Give students access to materials that are conducive to group work
     - Chart paper, markers, reference books, etc.
     - Boxes or tubs of project materials

2. Establishing *group routines* helps the classroom run smoothly and builds community at the same time. As you teach students how to manage grouping procedures, you are building students' capacity to work together as a community. Routines that build community include
   - Practice *transitioning* into and out of groups by drilling. Using a timer promotes efficiency in the transition time.
   - Establish *core groups* at the beginning of the year. These are groups of three to five students who stay together for at least a marking period. Core group members are responsible for homework help the first few minutes of class, catching group members up when they have missed work, and coming together to do quick oral reviews or during processing time. They look out for each other.

- Have *anchor activities* prepared. Anchor activities are specific activities that students move to automatically when they complete an assigned task. At the beginning of the year, we set an expectation in our classroom that if students are done early or they are waiting for us, they must work on an anchor activity. Anchor activities are meaningful tasks and self-correcting, not just busy work. They require no teacher direction. (See the "Resources" section for anchor activity ideas.)

3. Finally, it's the *positive emotional tone* in our classroom that brings our unique students together and builds community. Our message that, "This is our community; let's make it work together" creates a safe classroom and is demonstrated by . . .
   - Allowing groups of students to facilitate learning
   - Having students determine and set classroom expectations
   - Celebrating all learners by posting student work
   - Having students create bulletin boards
   - Facilitating team-building activities (See the "Resources" section for more information on team-building activities.)

Students must be taught to work in groups. We can't assume they come to us with prior experiences or understanding of how groups work. Some ways to help groups work well together are . . .

> We ought to think that we are one of the leaves of a tree, and the tree is all humanity. We cannot live without the others, without the tree.
>
> —Pablo Casals, Cellist

- Appointing jobs for each group member in a group. (Possible jobs: leader, recorder, time keeper, teacher getter, positive thinker, organizer)
- Brainstorming with students to develop expectations for working productively as a group. (Possible expectations: on task, sharing ideas, cooperating, using time wisely)
  - Create a rubric of criteria, and have each group assess itself at the end of each group work session. (See the "Resources" section for a group rubric template.)
  - Go around the room and agree or disagree with groups' self-assessment. You can include the group assessment as part of the grade for the project.
- Providing the class with feedback such as, "I really liked how DaShone's group was able to work through some of the problems members were having and to get back on track" or "I noticed some groups have members who are not clear on their responsibilities. Can we offer them some suggestions for solving that problem?"

Honoring our students, teaching them to thrive and to see their place in diverse learning communities, helps prepare our students for the future. Students who see themselves as contributing members of a classroom community will be prepared to enter the global community knowing they have their own unique talents to offer the world. They will also honor and respect that others have their place in the global community of the twenty-first century.

Just as we must teach our students to understand themselves, respect others, and work in a community, in the inspiring classroom we must also teach our students to own their learning. We want them to have that internal desire to pursue deeper understanding. To build this independence, we must teach our students, step by step, *how* to function independently. Chapter 4 explores how we can apprentice our students into becoming lifelong learners.

4

Creating Lifelong Learners

An Apprenticeship Approach

Much education today is monumentally ineffective. All too often we are giving young people cut flowers when we should be teaching them to grow their own plants.

—John W. Gardner

Imagine teaching teenagers how to drive by getting them to watch us drive cars and to take a quiz on the parts of a car and car safety— then expecting them to go out and drive a car. Would we feel safe on our roadways? No way! Instead, we teach teens to drive by offering them experiences in a progression toward independence. They begin by sitting next to us and watching us while we drive. We talk with them about how to drive. Then they take classes on the how-tos of driving followed by driving tests. Along the way, we encourage all approximations of driving. Teens practice driving and parking on back roads or in empty parking lots. Then, as their skills progress, we take them onto busier streets and finally highways. When we teach teenagers to drive, we apprentice them into that skill. We balance having them memorize facts with modeling and scaffolding instruction of skills; ultimately, we let them practice, practice, practice until they can drive on their own.

Maintaining a Balance

The successful teacher, who prepares students for life in and outside of school, approaches teaching with this same apprenticeship model in mind. Teaching this way involves a balanced approach of both traditional teaching methods and differentiated teaching methods. There *are* skills and information we need to teach our students directly and explicitly. Explicit teaching must be balanced with implicit learning experiences that allow students to own and have mastery of their learning.

Look at Figure 4.1. The teaching methods listed under "Traditional Teaching" will help students develop the skills they need to pass classes and obtain degrees. However, it is the teaching methods listed under "Differentiated Teaching" that will help students function independently and manage their lives on a day-to-day basis.

Let's reflect on the path we took to become educators as an example of why our students need to develop both sets of skills. We needed success with traditional methods to obtain a university degree in education and pass state certification exams. The skills we need to be a

Figure 4.1   A Comparison of Traditional and Differentiated Teaching

Traditional Teaching	Differentiated Teaching
Teacher-directed learning	Student-created learning
Teacher choice	Student choice
Test-taking skills	Products as assessment
Teacher feedback	Ongoing student self-assessment
Standards	Understandings
Teacher-established criteria	Constructivist
Rote learning	Active learning
Explicit teaching	Implicit teaching
Learning alone	Learning with a community
Following directions	Creating plans
Listening	Discussions
Teacher-generated questions	Student-generated inquiry
Sequential	Multitasking
Whole-group instruction	Small-group instruction for a variety of purposes *(readiness, special needs adaptations, interests, learning styles)*

truly effective teacher are much more complex. Our day-to-day success in the classroom requires differentiated skills such as multitasking, reflecting on our day's work, and creating plans for improving our teaching. Reading about these skills or taking a test does not develop these skills. These skills come from working with mentor teachers, collaborating with colleagues, teaching on our own, and reflecting on our teaching. *Both* the traditional learning and the life experiences create the balance needed for us to succeed in our work.

There is a time for traditional interactions with our students in which we are teachers and they are the learners. Eventually, however, if students are to take charge of their learning, our interactions need to shift to the mentor/apprentice model. We need to teach explicitly, then model and scaffold the traditional skills we want students to eventually own. Figure 4.2 illustrates and offers examples of the shift from traditional to differentiated interactions.

If our goal is to have students ask questions and construct meaning from investigations or texts, we must build those skills. We cannot assume that all students have mastered the skills of independent inquiry to the same degree, just as we would not assume that every 16-year-old has equivalent driving skills! Therefore, to move our students toward independence, our interactions must move along a continuum. When students

> *Insanity is doing the same things over and over again and expecting different results.*
>
> —Einstein

have no experience or knowledge, we must explicitly teach them the information. Next, we must help students practice the skills they

Figure 4.2   Stages: Moving Toward Independence

Traditional Interactions: Giving Explicit Instruction	Scaffolded Interactions: Developing Vital Know-Hows	Differentiated Interactions: Growing Student Independence
➤ Give information ➤ Teach and show ➤ Help students know or understand	➤ Conference and question ➤ Mentor and apprentice ➤ Help students own and apply independently	➤ Student-generated questions ➤ Students teaching others ➤ Students own and apply automatically
➤ Teach the components of a persuasive essay ➤ Explain the order of operations ➤ Tell students about key historical figures and dates ➤ Give directions for completing a lab, project, or report	➤ Model and generate persuasive writing together ➤ Demonstrate using the order of operations ➤ Students role-play and discuss events from history ➤ Conference with students about their progress	➤ Students use persuasion in real-life applications ➤ Students create story problems/answer keys for order of operations problems ➤ Use information from history to understand the world today ➤ Students make a plan for completing a project

need to become self-sufficient ("developing vital know-hows"). Here, we offer supportive coaching while students attempt tasks on their own. Finally, we need to let go and *expect* students to be able to work on their own. We remain present to offer assistance when problems arise.

Below are descriptions of five vital "know-hows" that students need most. Following the descriptions are the teaching methods that work most effectively in helping students develop those vital know-hows into lifelong learning tools.

Vital Know-Hows for Student Success

Vital Know-How #1: Reflective Learning

Definition: Reflective learning or metacognition is thinking about your own thinking and having a plan of action for what to do when you don't know.

Relevance: Learners who are self-reflective check to see if they are making sense of what they are learning, they assess what they know and still need to learn, and they reflect on what worked and what needs improving.

Ownership: Learners who are taught to be self-reflective increase the degree to which they are able to transfer their learning to new settings.

Vital Know-How #2: Discussion/Discourse

Definition: Discourse is the use of student-led conversations in order to deepen understanding. Learners take turns listening while other students verbally work through concepts and justify ideas.

Relevance: Learners who engage in discourse learn to listen to others, think deeply about their own ideas, and communicate effectively.

Ownership: Students who have skills in discourse can deepen their own understanding by constructing new meaning through conversations. They will be prepared to work collaboratively in the class and beyond.

Vital Know-How #3: Read/Write for Understanding

Definition: Strategic reading and writing skills are tools people use for processing and communicating understanding.

Relevance: Learners who have a toolkit of strategies for reading and writing are able to process and communicate more effectively in all subject areas. These skills need to be taught in all subject areas and grade levels (Biancarosa & Snow, 2006).

Ownership: Learners who read to understand can do the following:

Visualize what they are reading about

Sort important from interesting information

Ask good questions

Make connections between ideas

Recall what they have read

Evaluate and analyze new understandings

Self-monitor and adjust their thinking

Make inferences beyond the text

Learners who can write for understanding can do the following:

Take effective notes

Reflect on their understanding in logs or journals

Organize their thoughts into coherent written ideas

Write to learn, inform, persuade, and describe

Communicate their thoughts in a variety of writing genres

Vital Know-How #4: Inquiry/Research

Definition: Inquiry occurs when students ask thoughtful questions and determine ways to find answers to their questions.

Relevance: Learners who conduct long- or short-term research based on their own questions are able to search for answers, discover more, build knowledge, synthesize their thinking, and develop new insights.

Ownership: Learners who are involved in inquiry learn skills for answering their own questions and thus become more curious and engaged in their own learning.

Vital Know-How #5: Collaborative or Cooperative Learning

Definition: Collaborative learning is when students work effectively together on projects or tasks.

Relevance: The brain is a social brain and learns more effectively in a learning community than in isolation. (Two heads are better than one.)

Ownership: Students who learn the skills of collaboration will be able to work more effectively with others. This ability will help them not only in school but also in their personal relationships, in their careers, and in their communities.

How to Teach the Vital Know-Hows

When you plant lettuce, if it does not grow well, you don't blame the lettuce. You look into the reasons it is not doing well. It may need fertilizer, or more water, or less sun. You never blame the lettuce.

—Thich Nhat Hanh

To effectively apprentice students into owning these vital know-hows, we need to teach them through modeling/think alouds, explicit instruction, and scaffolding. Below is an explanation of each of these techniques, along with ideas for how to use them in your classroom.

Teach the Vital Know-Hows Through MODELING/THINK ALOUDS:

What it is:

You, the teacher, model aloud the metacognitive processes used for struggling with learning and for getting unstuck.

When modeling thinking about your learning, be sure to talk through how you monitor and adjust your thinking.

As students catch on to the idea of thinking aloud, have them talk through and share their processing.

Mental modeling helps students see how good learners comprehend what they are reading, develop writing ideas, solve problems, and so on.

How to do it:

Determine the skills that you want to model.

Think aloud the ways that you monitor and adjust your thinking to assess your understanding. (You may be modeling not only talk but also actions—i.e., drawing, writing, or moving—that you do to make sense of the learning.)

As students catch on, ask them to share other ways they may have gotten to the same understanding.

Figure 4.3   Inspiring Image: Think Aloud

What It Looks Like	What It Sounds Like
Ms. Alberson stands at the overhead with sample text displayed. Students observe the teacher, and they listen as she works through a difficult piece of text and talks about her thinking. The teacher makes notes about her thinking and about her reading for students to see.	"As I'm reading this text about pruning trees, I notice that it refers to 'hardwoods' and that makes me start to wonder if the tree that I need to prune would fall into this category. I'm going to make a note here in the margin that means I need to find out more information about this."

Teach the Vital Know-Hows Through EXPLICIT INSTRUCTION:

What it is:

Explicit teaching involves breaking down a learning task into small parts or steps and teaching each of those steps individually through explanation, demonstration, modeling/thinking aloud, and student practice.

Explicit teaching provides guided instruction for students in learning new topics or skills. Students then elaborate on their new learning through discourse, practice, writing, and the like.

How to do it: The steps for explicit teaching are as follows:

Set a purpose for learning. (Make it relevant!)

Tell students what to do step by step.

Show them step by step how to do it.

Monitor their application of the new learning.

Figure 4.4   Inspiring Image: Explicit Instruction

What It Looks Like	What It Sounds Like
Mr. Eton writes on the board "Two-Column Notes" and underneath writes, "SO WHAT? Why should I learn to do this Mr. E?"	"We are learning to take two-column notes today. This strategy is a great way to help you make more sense of anything you read. It can be used for textbook reading, for things you enjoy reading, and maybe even someday in your jobs. You can get a lot of mileage out of this strategy in several different places so it's a great one to be able to do. So, I'm going to show you step by step how to do this. First, if you make two columns and add a heading, that will help you determine . . . "

Teach the Vital Know-Hows Through SCAFFOLDING:

What it is:

When teaching a new concept or strategy, the teacher realizes that students need a great deal of support.

Through modeling and explicit teaching, the teacher creates a safe environment for learning the new information until the students begin to ask self-regulatory questions about their learning.

As the teacher sees that students are "getting it," the teacher gradually removes the support to allow students to try their independence. (Pearson & Gallagher, 1983)

Some students may still be unable to achieve independence, so the teacher brings back the support system to help those students experience success until they are able to achieve independence. (For more information on scaffolding, see Collins, Brown, & Newman, 1989; Vygotsky, 1978).

How to do it:

- Present the new strategy.
  - Model the skill
  - Think out loud while you or the students make decisions
  - EXAMPLE: *"Today we are going to be talking about 'reflecting.' This skill is absolutely essential for anything you do, whether it's school work, a craft or project, or even working with other people. When you reflect, you look back at your work and decide what was working and what you would change if you did it again. I'm going to show you how I would reflect on my own work. Let's look at this paper that I wrote a long time ago when I was in college."*

- Monitor and adjust difficulty during guided practice.
  - Start with less complex information and gradually increase the complexity
  - Complete part of the task for the students
  - Present the material in small steps
  - EXAMPLE: *"Here are three things I want you to reflect on today: what were you successful at, examples that show your successes, and what was new or surprising to you?"*

- Provide a variety of ways for students to practice.
  - Provide teacher-led practice
  - Students engage in reciprocal teaching
  - Students work in small groups
  - EXAMPLE: *"You are going to be working in a small group today to reflect on yesterday's homework. I'd like you to talk to your partner about how you feel you are doing. Your partner's job is to*

ask you questions to help you reflect deeper. Partners, you need to come up with the questions you want your partner to reflect on."

- Offer regular feedback.
  - o Provide teacher and student feedback
  - o Design checklists for self-reflection
  - o Share models of expert work
  - o EXAMPLE: *"I really like the questions that Susie was asking. I noticed that some people were not really giving specific examples in the reflection—it was pretty general. As a partner, be aware of that and try to request an example that will help your partner go deeper."*

- Increase student responsibility (as students show they can do it).
  - o Begin to diminish prompts and models
  - o Gradually increase complexity and difficulty of information
  - o Gradually decrease student support
  - o EXAMPLE: *"OK, we've been practicing being more self-reflective. I'm handing back yesterday's work, and I'd like you to write reflections about the work you've done on this 3 × 5 card. You might want to consider looking at quality or how your thinking has changed."*

- Provide independent practice.
  - o Provide extensive practice opportunities
  - o Help students to apply and transfer the learning to new situations
  - o EXAMPLE: *"OK, we've been practicing being more self-reflective. Tonight for homework I would like you to do a quick write. I would like you to reflect on this question, 'How has reflecting helped me to become a better learner?' Yes, I get it. You are reflecting on reflecting!"*

Modeling, explicitly teaching, and scaffolding the five vital know-hows will help students to take ownership of their learning. Of course students cannot master all of these skills immediately. Just like learning to hit a baseball or play an expert game of chess, mastering lifelong learning tools requires continual coaching and practice. This means that teachers in all grade levels and all subject areas need to teach the vital know-hows. The best teaching is a balance between explicitly teaching vital skills, encouraging students to own new learning, and seeing that students can reflect on their growth. The apprenticeship model of teaching sends students out of our classrooms with lifelong learning tools; *they* are in the driver's seat!

In the next three chapters, we will look at "Lite-n-Lean Strategies," "Deep and Dynamic Lesson Designs," and "Assessment Tools" that allow students to practice independence and ownership of their own learning. (For a bibliography on how to teach vital know-hows, see the "Resources" section.)

Sometimes one sees in the school simply the instrument for transferring a certain maximum quantity of knowledge to the growing generation.

But that is not right.

Knowledge is dead.

The school, however, serves the living.

It should develop in the young individuals those qualities and capabilities which are of value for the welfare of the commonwealth.

But that does not mean that individuality should be destroyed and the individual become a mere tool of the community, like a bee or an ant.

For a community of standardized individuals without personal originality and personal aims would be a poor community without possibilities for development.

On the contrary, the aim must be the training of independently acting and thinking individuals, who, however, see in the service of the community their highest life problem.

—Albert Einstein, 1936

PART II

Activities and Designs to Inspire Middle and Secondary Learners

5

Lite-n-Lean
Learning
Activities

Beginning Steps for Inspiring Learners

The vision must be followed by the venture. It is not enough to stare up the steps—we must step up the stairs.
—Vance Havner

In Chapter 4, we learned how to explicitly teach our students the vital know-hows they need to become lifelong learners. In this chapter, we will look at instructional strategies we can use to respond to students' differences and apprentice them into knowing themselves as learners. With our core beliefs firmly in place, let's take a look at some lite-n-lean activities designed and used by real teachers. These approaches are a great way to begin intentionally responding to our learners' needs. They are easy to do and students enjoy them. These activities are a starting point to help us build a foundation for designing the dynamic lessons that will allow us to teach the state standards in a meaningful way to the various learners that sit before us (Chapter 6).

First, let's begin by recalling the five elements teachers can differentiate when designing lessons to meet students' needs:

Chunk: How students take in information

Chew: How students make sense of information

Check: How students show what they know

The Environment: The tone and routines of the classroom

The Information: What students learn

Figure 5.1 Five Elements We Can Differentiate

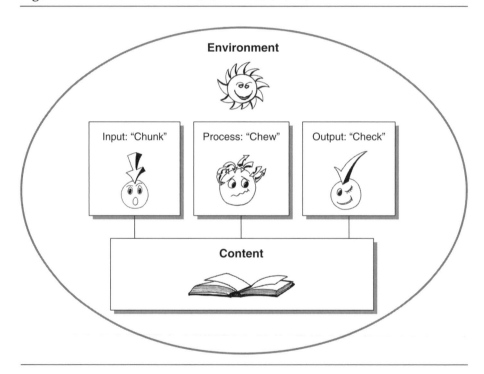

Many of us already differentiate at least one, if not more, of these elements. However, the key to moving forward in our practice is to know *why* we are doing what we are doing. It is not enough to just randomly do activities or apply strategies. Students will be inspired by us when we share with them that we have thought about their needs and designed lessons as a response to what they need.

Note: Each lite-n-lean activity will include an informational key that notes what we intended to differentiate in the lesson.

Investigations for Advanced Learners

❑ Chunk/Information Acquired	According to	❑ Learning Profile
❑ Chew/Information Processed		❑ Student Interests
❑ Check/Information Out		☒ Readiness
☒ The Information		

Beyond asking advanced learners to think about ideas in a hierar-chy of thinking levels, consider offering challenges that are multifac-eted, such as those listed below:

Connecting to Other Subject Matter

What was happening in art at this time?

How does this relate or connect to science?

What is the math behind this idea?

How can we use language arts to help clarify our math thinking?

Issues Throughout Time: Past, Present, Future

Was this an issue in the past?

How did this come to be?

When was this discovered? What effects did this discovery have?

How might this be different in the future?

What issues today could affect this in the future?

Questions of Principle

Is this point of view right or wrong?

What values govern this idea?

Who would do this?

Would you do this?

How is this good for humans?

How does this affect other living things?

Point of View

What is your point of view?

What would a character's point of view be?

What would be the point of view from someone in another field?

Advanced students could use these as an anchor activity, a short- or long-term project, or an independent investigation.

Questions for Discussions and Journaling

	According to	
❑ Chunk/Information Acquired		❑ Learning Profile
❑ Chew/Information Processed		❑ Student Interests
☒ Check/Information Out		☒ Readiness
❑ The Information		

When we introduce classroom discussions, it is important to start with questions that all students can answer and then move to more challenging questions to offer some students the opportunity to think more deeply about the content. These questions can be used to initiate classroom discussions or as prompts for journal entries. Sometimes it's a good idea to have students springboard from journal responses into classroom discussions. This can be done with students grouped at various readiness levels.

Offering Students Choices

	According to	
❑ Chunk/Information Acquired		☒ Learning Profile
❑ Chew/Information Processed		❑ Student Interests
☒ Check/Information Out		❑ Readiness
❑ The Information		

One of the easiest ways to honor students' different learning styles is to give them choices. Secondary students respond powerfully when they are able to select how they will share what they learned. You can introduce choice in a variety of ways. We will look at choices in homework, tests, and studying vocabulary.

Figure 5.2   Questioning for Increasing Challenge

Fact Question Who, What, Where, When, Why	Locate and define (five) important terms . . .
Describe/Retell Question What happened? Summarize in your own words . . .	Give an example that illustrates . . .

Relevance Question
Why is this important to you/your world?
Discuss reasons that . . .
Make a list of questions you might want
   to ask someone . . .
	Make a list of important ideas that you would
	   include in a discussion of a topic of your choice.

Same-or-Different Question How are these the same? How are they different? What are the pros and cons of . . .	What was the cause of . . . What was the result of . . .
Creation Question What would happen if . . .? Imagine that . . . Create . . .	Invent something that . . . Name it, describe it, formulate it Transform . . .
Judge Question What is the best way to . . .? Support or criticize . . .	Convince . . . Defend . . . Convince . . .

1. Choices on Homework

Surface Area Homework Assignment

Choose from one of the following items, so that you can *best* apply what you have learned in class today. This will be due tomorrow for 10 points.

Imagine that you have become weightless and can float above your bedroom. Draw a picture of the furniture that you see. Give imaginary dimensions (be sure to use UNITS), and find the area of at least three pieces of furniture.

Using the graph paper and markers provided on the back table, cut out rectangles of various sizes and color with vibrant patterns. On the back of each rectangle, show how your friend could

> If students are to be predominately self-motivated, they must be given the opportunity to focus on their own areas of interest and participate in activities they find interesting.
>
> — Eric Jensen

determine the area of that object. (Hint: Remember that each square is a centimeter long and wide.)

Complete the problems on page 256 in Check for Understanding, #8–18.

Create a poem describing a beautiful handwoven rug from India and how the weaver could find out the area that it will cover.

2. Choices on Tests

This is the end of a high school science chapter test created by S. Joy Stephens. The rest of the test is multiple choice, fill in the blank, and short answer.

Science Test: Animal Kingdom

Choose one of the following activities below to show what you have learned in this chapter. (5 points each)

Create an imaginary organism that will fit in one of the kingdoms EXCEPT the animal kingdom. Draw a picture of that organism. Tell what major characteristics it has in order to be placed in the kingdom you chose.

Write a short letter to an archaeologist describing briefly what you have learned about fossils and geology. Include several questions that you may have developed while studying this chapter that he or she could answer.

Develop five questions that could appear on "Who Wants to Be a Millionaire?" They should be about topics that were NOT covered on this test but are related to this chapter.

Create a rhyme that you could teach to a middle school student so that she or he could remember the categories of classification (all seven).

Think about a walk in the woods. List seven things you might encounter, and describe how you would begin to classify them. Be as specific as possible.

3. Choices for Vocabulary

Vocabulary Menu

Understand: We all learn in different ways and, therefore, need to find ways of studying that work successfully for our learning style.

Know: Key vocabulary terms for the unit

Do: Practice your vocabulary in a way that matches your learning style.

Activity: Study the key vocabulary using the process indicated on the next page that best matches your learning style.

Draw vocabulary pictures.

Your Choice:
Come up with your own unique way to study your vocabulary words. (You must get the okay from your teacher first!)

Create a rap, song, or poem using your vocabulary words.

Act out your vocabulary words.

Work with a study partner to say, hear, and coach each other on the vocabulary words.

Weekly Vocabulary Choices

30 points = A   25 points = B   20 points = C

- Make a set of flash cards for studying your words. (10 pts)
- Practice reviewing the words and their meanings with a family member or friend. (5 pts)
- Create a song or rhyme for each vocabulary word. (15 pts)
- Draw a picture that shows your understanding of each word. (15 pts)
- Write sentences that show you understand the meaning of each word. Underline the word. (10 pts)
- Use a tape recorder to practice words. State each word, give the definition, and then spell it. (10 pts)
- Create a word game (bingo, word search, crossword, charades, or make fill-ins). (15 pts)
- Create a word wall bulletin board with descriptions of each word. (15pts)
- Classify the words according to the parts of speech (grammar books are available). (10 pts)
- Write a story using all the words (correct paragraph format). Underline the vocabulary words. (15 pts)
- Write a synonym and an antonym for each word. (15 pts)
- Use your words in poetry. Underline the words. (15 pts)
- Write newspaper headlines using your words. (15 pts)
- Create a word map for each word. Use at least four categories. (If you include a description of the word, then you can count that as your 15 points for describing the word. See list of map ideas.) (15–30 pts)
- Create your own activity. (15 pts) [Ask for approval from the teacher.]

Graphic Organizers

	According to	
☒ Chunk/Information Acquired		☒ Learning Profile
❑ Chew/Information Processed		❑ Student Interests
❑ Check/Information Out		❑ Readiness
❑ The Information		

Teachers today know that graphic organizers are powerful learning tools to use in classroom instruction. (In this book, we define graphic organizers as any visual diagram such as cluster maps, webbing, KWL charts, Venn diagrams, or brainstorming charts.) Some of the benefits of using graphic organizers include the following:

Activates students' thinking

Helps students retrieve prior knowledge

Links new information with the old (This is how the brain learns best!)

Assists students in retaining and transferring knowledge

Allows students to visualize the learning process

Graphic organizers are excellent learning tools to use for all learners if they are used in meaningful and engaging ways. Students will quickly tire of them if they become the next dittoed worksheet, or if students are not taught to see the relevance of using graphic representations. For example, students need to know that people in corporate boardrooms in America are using mind maps and brainstorm maps to plan and organize their thinking. (Bet they don't fill them out as dittos, either!) If you are doing a KWL with your students, do they know that this is modeling what good readers do before, during, and after learning? Graphic organizers should be living, breathing documents that are created by the students for the students' needs as learners.

Following are some suggestions for using graphic organizers in ways that increase students' engagement and understanding.

Make the graphic organizers *big* and *alive*. Use chart paper and markers. Have students work in groups of three to brainstorm ideas. Have them post their graphic organizers around the room for other students to see. Allow groups to walk around the room and look at other groups' graphic organizers. Have them bring along a clipboard and appoint a recorder, so they can write down any information that they didn't include on their map. Then, when they return back to their own maps, they can add the information they learned from their peers.

Don't run off organizers as dittos! Instead, make an overhead model of a graphic organizer and model on the overhead how this structure helps you to organize your thinking. Allow students to create their own visual maps as long as these meet the criteria you are asking for in the lesson. Students who want to use your framework may do so. You can also have some copies of your map for students who really struggle with developing their own schema.

Use graphic organizers to chart and show growth in the learning process. At the end of a marking period, put up chart paper with a circle in the middle that states, "What we learned in (*subject area*) this marking period." As students share things they have learned, write the information on the chart and put each student's initials under his or her comment. (Students love seeing their names on the charts.) Create a new map each marking period. Take previous quarters' maps out, and add the new ones so students can see how much they have grown as learners. This is especially powerful for struggling learners because they don't visualize themselves as learners.

Some students struggle with finding main ideas or categories to use when organizing information in their cluster maps. Give those students what they need to succeed by giving them a list of the categories of information to include on their map. Challenge the more advanced students to find their own categories.

Students love creating graphic organizers on computers. This adds novelty, and the learning brain loves novelty. Some quality computer programs for graphic organizers are Inspiration and Kidspiration. (PS: These programs are easy to use!)

Mapping is an excellent strategy for learning vocabulary. Vocabulary maps allow students to explore a word in various ways.

Students can create their own vocabulary maps, or they can work with a partner or small group to create maps. Have students keep a vocabulary journal in a spiralbound notebook or composition book. This will give students a log of their vocabulary learning and will also keep you away from the copy machine!

Groups can create a map for different words and then teach each other their words using their maps. Keep the maps posted in the room so that students can keep learning from them.

Teachers can assign one or two "Must Do" categories and then allow students to choose two categories of their own.

Some categories for vocabulary mapping may include the following (teachers should select several categories that are appropriate for the age and subject level they are teaching):

Guess the meaning (prefixes, suffixes, root words)

What is it?/Describe the word

Antonyms/Opposite words

Synonyms/Related words

Analogies/Similes/Metaphors (This is like . . .)

Examples from text (number problems, experiments, etc.)

Examples from life

TV/Movie examples

Use word in a sentence

Connections to related concepts

Pictures/Drawing

Figure 5.3   Examples of Graphic Organizers for Vocabulary

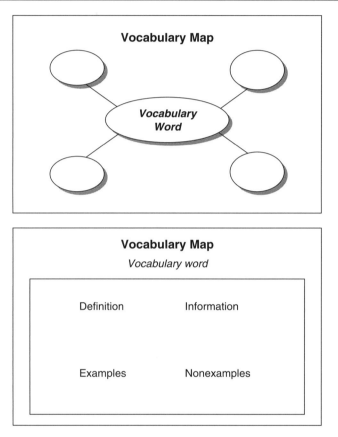

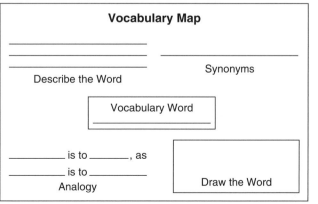

Vocabulary Instruction for Different Learning Profiles

❏ Chunk/Information Acquired	According to	☒ Learning Profile
❏ Chew/Information Processed		❏ Student Interests
☒ Check/Information Out		❏ Readiness
❏ The Information		

In any subject area, new learning is more likely to occur if students comprehend key vocabulary. It is essential that we teach vocabulary in ways that are meaningful to the *variety* of learners in our classrooms. When we were in school, most likely the teacher had us copy the words and the definitions, memorize them, and then take a test. This strategy worked well for many of us, so we are still using it in our classrooms today. But, as you have probably discovered, the reality is that this strategy works well for *some*, but not *most* of today's learners. Gifted students think that copying and memorizing definitions is a waste of time. They may refuse to do the assignment. Struggling learners spend hours painstakingly copying the words and definitions, but they may not have a clue what they have written! Basically, teaching vocabulary through rote memorization lends itself to input/output learning. Students quickly memorize vocabulary for the test, take the test, and then forget the information shortly thereafter. To teach vocabulary for deep meaning, we need to teach to a variety of learning styles.

Here's another idea we need to keep in mind. Just because textbook publishers bold-faced words in a text doesn't mean we are required to have students learn them. Textbooks are written for the purpose of selling them to the masses, so they highlight many words. When we try to teach too many key words to students, we will end up doing quantity (input/output) teaching rather than quality (engaging/ meaningful) teaching. To determine which words we really need to teach students, we need to look at our curriculum, think about our objectives, and then determine what vocabulary our students most need to know to reach deep understanding of the content. Think about it. We will buy more time to do powerful teaching of vocabulary if we teach 5–10 words deeply as opposed to 10–20 words superficially.

We need to remember that the goal is to help students discover how they learn best. So, as we teach the different approaches for learning vocabulary, we must explain what learning styles the strategies address. Students should be looking for the strategies that work best for them, and they should know to study this way at home as well as in other classes. If we send them out into the world with their own personal tools for making meaning out of new words, we have truly empowered them for a lifetime.

Here are some tried-and-true ideas for teaching vocabulary in ways that have meaning for all types of learners. Each lesson has a key showing which learning styles we are tapping into when we teach this way.

Learning Style Key		
S = See it	W = Write or Draw it	
H = Hear it	T = Touch it	
M = Move it	Sp = Speak it	

1. **Picture Words** (S/T/W): Students draw pictures or graphics that represent vocabulary words. EXAMPLE:

Fold sheets of 11 × 14 inch white construction paper into squares and have students draw a picture on each square. Rachel, a special education student who loved this strategy, suggested cutting the picture words into squares and then writing the words and descriptions of the words on the back, thus creating study flash cards. Great idea!

Have students make booklets of vocabulary drawings.

Get chart paper, put students in groups of three, give them one word to draw a representation for, then tape the charts around the room and have other students guess which word is represented. Now we're teaching to even more learning styles.

2. **Kiddie Vocabulary** (S/Sp/W): Have students work in pairs to rewrite vocabulary words in ways that a much younger student could understand. For example, here is the eighth grade science word *resistance* with a second grade definition: *When you don't want to do what your mommy wants you to do.*

3. **Vocabulary Bingo** (S/H/Sp/T): This is a great way to review for a test. Have students create their own bingo cards with key vocabulary

written on them. Read sentences that leave out the vocabulary word. For example, "*A ___ economy is based on supply and demand.*" Students fill in the vocabulary word on their bingo cards as you read. When a student gets a "bingo," he or she must read the complete sentences for each of the words. In this way, the entire class hears the correct answers each time there is a winner.

4. **Vocabulary Anticipation Guides** (IS/H/W): Create true-or-false sentences about the vocabulary words. Students predict the meaning of each definition by placing a "T" or "F" for each definition. Prepare students to read for meaning and discover the true definitions by looking for context clues and word clues such as prefixes and suffixes and root words. When students read the text assignment, they will be more engaged in the reading as they verify their predictions. After reading the text, go back and discuss the guide and rewrite incorrect answers so that students remember the correct meanings.

5. **Vocabulary Charades** (M/Sp): Put students in groups of two or three. Groups should create actions that represent their vocabulary words. Each group performs a charade of these vocabulary words for the class to guess.

6. **Matching Cards** (S/T/M/W/Sp): Give students strips of card stock. (Cut three strips out of an 8 1/2 × 11 piece of card stock). On one half, the students write the vocabulary word, and, on the other half, they write definitions in their own words. Then students make their cards into puzzle-like pieces by cutting the cards in half with patterns such as zigzags, curves, or true puzzle shapes. Students can exchange card sets and study from another student's set, or they can quiz each other.

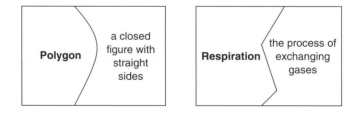

7. **Vocabulary Learning Stations** (S/H/M/W/T/Sp): Set up three or four different learning stations with a different vocabulary strategy at each station; for example, vocabulary pictures, vocabulary charades, and matching cards. Students rotate though the stations in groups. Be sure to ask students which strategies work best for their learning styles.

8. **Ball Toss** (S/H/M/Sp): Have students sit on their desks. Put a vocabulary word on the overhead. Toss a Nerf or Koosh ball to a student and ask for the meaning of the word. If the student can give you the definition, he or she throws the ball to the next student. If the student doesn't know the word, he or she returns the ball to you to select another student. Repeat!

9. **Moving Matching Cards** (S/H/M/Sp): Using a stack of index cards, write vocabulary words on some cards and the matching definition on others. Shuffle the cards. Pass out one card to each student. Students must move around the room silently to find people with cards that match their own. Students line up around the room with their matches. Replay as time allows.

Learning Profile Projects

	According to	
❏ Chunk/Information Acquired		☒ Learning Profile
❏ Chew/Information Processed		❏ Student Interests
❏ Check/Information Out		❏ Readiness
☒ The Information		

When grouping students for learning profile projects, we can group them by the same or similar learning profiles, allowing students to grow their skills with others who have similar strengths. We can also group students by varied learning profiles to give students an opportunity to have their skills complemented or to create projects that are more multifaceted. The activities that follow are designed for students grouped with others having similar learning profiles.

Scientific Method Mnemonics

Your Assignment:

- Get in groups of three by your strongest intelligence.
- Create a memory trick that would assist someone with your intelligence strength in remembering the steps of the scientific method.
- Share your creation with the rest of the class.

The Steps of the Scientific Method

Problem (Purpose)

Hypothesis (Because)

Experiment (Test)

Analyze (Think numbers!)

Conclude

Scientific Method Mnemonics Rubric

Expectations	Bill Nye is jealous!	Pretty good!	Not bad, but no prize	Dr. Science, you are not
Quality (As defined by YOU!) Points: 10	Top quality 9–10	Good quality 7–8	Fair quality 5–6	Needs better quality 0–4
Represented all steps of scientific method in a creative way Points: 30	All steps are there and very creative 25–30	All steps and rather creative 20–25	Steps missing and minimal creativity 15–20	Steps missing and little creativity 10–15
Used time wisely and worked well in your group Points: 10	Superb 9–10	Standard 7–8	So-so 5–6	Slipped 0–4
What we did that was quality work:	What we would do differently next time:			

Student Grade _____   Teacher Grade _____

Teacher Comments:

Adding Fractions Mnemonics

Your Assignment:

- Get in groups of three.
- Create a memory trick that would assist someone in remembering the steps of adding fractions.
- Share your creation with the rest of the class.

The Steps of Adding Fractions

Find the COMMON DENOMINATOR.

To do that, find the LOWEST COMMON MULTIPLE. (If all else fails, simply multiply the two denominators together.)

Now, make the two fractions EQUIVILENT FRACTIONS.

Add the NUMERATORS.

Simplify the fraction.

Adding Fractions Mnemonics Rubric

Expectations	Great job!	Pretty good!	Not bad, but no prize	Not so hot
Quality (As defined by YOU!) Points:	Top quality _____	Good quality _____	Fair quality _____	Needs better quality _____
Showed all steps of adding fractions method in a creative way Points:	All steps there and very creative _____	All steps and rather creative _____	Steps missing and minimal creativity _____	Steps missing and little creativity _____
Used time wisely and worked well in your group Points:	Superb _____	Standard _____	So-so _____	Slipped _____
What we did that was quality work:	What we would do differently next time:			

Student Grade _____   Teacher Grade _____

Teacher Comments:

Interest-Based Projects

Chunk/Information Acquired	According to	Learning Profile
☐ Chunk/Information Acquired	According to	☐ Learning Profile
☐ Chew/Information Processed		☒ Student Interests
☐ Check/Information Out		☐ Readiness
☒ The Information		

A fun and easy way to get students engaged in learning is to let them work in groups on interest-based projects. When teaching a new unit, we can begin by preassessing using an interest inventory to find out what content within the unit students are most interested in studying. Allow students to group together as they become experts in their area of interest. Each group then shares with the rest of the class what its members have learned. Some examples of interest-based groups in content areas might include the following:

Science:

Endangered Species—Group by the species they are most interested in studying

Newton's Laws—Students group by the law they are interested in exploring

History/Geography:

Holocaust—Students do an in-depth study of an area they are most interested in, such as the Nazi movement, Poland, or the ghettos.

Geography—When students are studying regions, let them become experts in regions that they most want to explore

Language Arts/English:

Literary Circles—Students do "Book Club" literary circles around books they have selected. You could also teach a literary concept such as internal conflict by letting students find examples in stories that they select to read in interest groups

Writing Genres—Let students create magazines or newsletters by collaborating in groups based on the genre of writing they would like to do (e.g., feature story, advice column, recipes, editorials)

Math

Geometry—Students work in interest-based groups to study everyday applications of geometry

Consumer Math—Students work in groups to study different types of savings or investment plans

Health/Physical Education

Health Awareness—Students collaborate in groups around teenage health topics of interest

Personal Fitness—Students have days when they can group together to do fitness activities of their choice (weight lifting, aerobics, jogging/walking, basketball, etc.)

Varying Text Levels

☒ Chunk/Information Acquired	According to	☒ Learning Profile
☐ Chew/Information Processed		☐ Student Interests
☐ Check/Information Out		☐ Readiness
☐ The Information		

Would you be shocked to hear that students in a single class have a wide range of reading abilities? Hardly! As teachers, we live this reality every day. In an ideal world, all students in one grade or class would read at the same level, but this is an unrealistic and unfair view of how the world should be. When would we expect all 16-year-old students to sing equally as well? Why would we expect all 14-year-olds to grow physically to equal heights? Yet reading, or the linguistic intelligence, is sometimes viewed as a talent that should come equally as easily for all students. It's just unrealistic. What do we do as teachers to meet the needs of these students who are just plain different from one another?

It is essential that we have texts available at various levels, such as textbooks, short essays, and magazine and informational articles related to lessons. You are most likely thinking, *"Where am I supposed to get the money and time to supply my class with varying texts?"* First, give yourself some time. Below are suggestions for how to begin.

How to Get Started Collecting Texts of Various Levels

Begin with a topic that seems most difficult for students of varying abilities to understand. If we add one or two resource options for this topic every year, our collection will add up quickly.

With permission, keep papers written by students. Add these to the collection of resource material for a topic.

Do an Internet search for the topic that needs additional support. Add "children" or "elementary" to your search for information written at less complex levels. The Internet is also a great resource for information for more advanced students.

Call a local library and have librarians pull resources on your topic.

If your building has a classroom wish list for the PTA or back-to-school time, add the resources to this list.

See the Resources for a list of publishers that offer high interest/low level texts for content area instruction.

Ask your special education staff or gifted/talented coordinator for ideas and resources.

How to Use Texts of Various Levels

Set clear objectives by having one set of questions you want all students to explore, questions that focus on the big idea. You can dis-

tribute the resources to groups of students at varied readiness levels, or you can allow students to select from the varied resources. Model through think alouds the value of finding information from several valid resources. This will allow students to explore texts at various levels with more freedom.

Memory Techniques

☒ Chunk/Information Acquired	According to	☒ Learning Profile
❑ Chew/Information Processed		❑ Student Interests
❑ Check/Information Out		❑ Readiness
❑ The Information		

The brain learns and recalls information in a variety of ways. Here are some great memory strategies for all learners.

Copy Change: Copy change is simply taking a piece of text or a song and having students use the pattern of that writing to help them remember content from our subject area. For example, to remember the water cycle, students can learn this song, which is sung to the tune of "Oh My Darling, Clementine."

Condensation, evaporation, precipitation on my mind

They are part of the water cycle

And they're changing all the time!

Students can work together to create their own songs to help them recall content. We can record the best songs and keep a collection of them for students to use as a learning resource in the future.

Total Physical Response: Movement helps the brain to recall information. Total Physical Response (TPR) (Asher, 2000) is creating movements that help students remember content in your subject area. For example, if you are teaching the parts of a letter (heading, greeting, body, closing, signature), have the students stand up. Then have them pat their heads with their hands and say "heading," wave "hello" as they say "greeting," rub their stomachs as they say "body," stomp their feet as they say "closing," and write an imaginary signature in the air as they say "signature." TPR may seem silly at first, but once you see how well it works in helping students recall information, you'll be movin' and groovin' in your classroom.

Interactive Note Taking: Create note taking guides or graphic organizers that allow students to interact and be more focused during classroom presentations. When graphic organizers are used this way, it's okay to copy forms for students. To use these interactive guides, give students a form that includes the key ideas that you will be discussing. The students will fill the information in as they hear or learn about it. When we give students an organizer like one of those shown below, with key ideas outlined, we can let students chunk and chew differently. They can listen to a lecture, read the text, or listen to the text read on a CD or cassette. Our wrap-up discussion is focused on the key ideas provided in the outline to ensure that our learners stay focused on the important information. We can allow students to work alone or with a partner and even to draw or write their notes to add information to the interactive organizers. Here are two examples:

Figure 5.4   Two Examples of Graphic Organizers

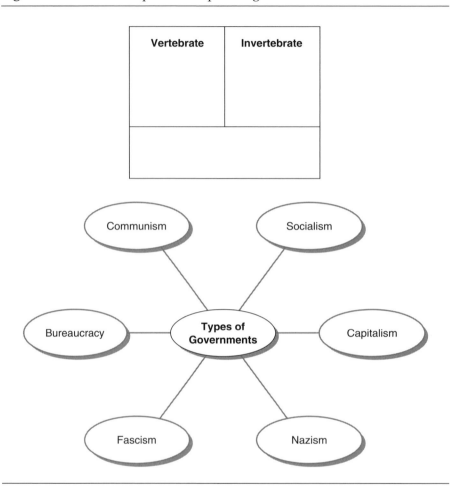

Designing lessons that keep our learners engaged is vital to providing effective instruction. The data we collect about our learners, whether on their personal interests, learning styles, or environmental preferences, will help provide a road map that guides us when differentiating the various classroom elements that will meet our learners' needs. Our next step to truly inspiring our learners is to develop lessons that not only honor our students' learning needs, but offer meaningful ways to meet our teaching targets.

6

Teaching for Meaning

Enduring understandings provide a larger purpose for learning targeted content. They implicitly answer the question, "Why is this worth knowing?"

—Jay McTighe

The brain understands best when it sees the learning as relevant. In this chapter, you will learn to design your lessons using our C U KAN framework to ensure that your lessons are engaging and connected to the lives of your students, and also help students attain curriculum objectives.

What Is C U KAN?

We like to pronounce it "See, you can!" to help us remember the important components of meaningful lessons. C U KAN is an acronym for the essential outcomes of learning (Figure 6.1). When planning a unit or lesson, this framework will help us clarify the objectives, or learning target, for the lesson. Our framework is adapted from the work of Grant Wiggins, Jay McTighe, and Carol Ann Tomlinson.

Figure 6.1   C U KAN Components

Concept

The **Concept** is the big overarching idea of a unit or lesson. The concept is *not* the topic of the lesson, such as "multiplying fractions" or "photosynthesis." It is very global, broad, and can be applied across subject areas. The concept is usually one word such as "change" or "relationships."

Understand (that)

The **Understandings** are the underlying principles embedded within the concepts. Understandings answer the question, "Why is it important to know this?" and help us connect the content to students' lives. When we develop understandings for our lessons, adding the word "that" (*Understand that . . .*) helps us move away from teaching just facts and knowledge toward teaching the big ideas that are the heart of our subject, such as, "Understand that change happens over time."

Know

The **Know** comprises the key facts and key vocabulary that enable students to speak to the understandings. They are often examples of the understandings, or facts related to the understandings. The facts are content specific, such as, "The African culture is changing due to the AIDS epidemic" or "Frodo changed when he left Middle Earth."

Able to Do

The **Able to do** skills are the social skills, production skills, fundamental skills, or skills of the discipline that students need to be able to do as they work toward the understandings. **Able to do** targets might be "how to work in groups," "how to read a chart," or "how to take notes for research."

Now You Get It!

The **Now you get it** is the way that students demonstrate understanding (transfer) of the targeted learning objectives. The **Now you get it** can occur during and after learning by using exit cards, tests and quizzes, and various performance-based assessments.

Why C U KAN?

Designing engaging and meaningful lessons becomes effective and efficient when we use the C U KAN framework. The C U KAN framework lets us begin with the end in mind and helps us do the following:

1. C U KAN provides a target for meaningful learning.

For Us: If we want students to be engaged in our content and lessons, we must design lessons that connect to our students and their world. The C U KAN framework points out global applications, underlying principles, and key important information that will help us connect to the brain's need for relevance.

For Our Students: Our students want to know and deserve to know how the content we teach connects to their world. Using the C U KAN framework allows us to give a meaningful response to the question, "Why do we have to know this?" We will be able to respond to students by explaining. Here is an example: "Exponents are mathematical shortcuts that help us write large numbers more efficiently. That's important because it allows us to spend our time using the math to answer interesting and useful questions, such as how far it is from Earth to Venus or how many blood cells there are in the average human body, rather than on computing." With meaningful learning targets students, will know how the learning connects to their lives.

2. C U KAN provides a target for meaningful instruction.

For Us: Being clear about the learning target before we write our daily lessons ensures that the activities we design to *Chunk, Chew,* and *Check* our lessons are really hitting our target and are not simply busy work. A clear learning target helps us to plan instructional options that reach all our students. For example, we can plan for students who need information visually, students who learn best through discussions, or students who need language support. The C U KAN framework also frees us from teaching to the book. It helps us discern what parts of the book support the learning target and when other resources would better hit the target. For example, we don't need to teach 20 vocabulary terms just because our textbook has 20 bold-faced vocabulary terms in Chapter 3. A clear learning target allows us to make better choices about which words our students most need to know in order to deeply understand, apply, and transfer the learning.

For Our Students: When the learning target is clear, our students can shift their thinking from, "What am I supposed to be learning?" to,

"What is the best way for me to learn this?" How can students possibly select a learning strategy to help them hit the target when they don't know what the target is? A clear learning target allows students to use their time more efficiently by studying in a way that works for them.

3. C U KAN provides a target for meaningful assessment.

For Us: Our assessment options become clear when we ask, "How can students best demonstrate that they understand the learning target?" When we know our target and we know our students, we can better determine whether to offer choices, tier our lessons, or let students do independent learning contracts. We can also save ourselves valuable class time by preassessing to determine what our students already know or don't know about the learning target. This information helps us to prioritize our time and focus on what students really need to learn.

For Our Students: Clear learning targets help our students reflect on and assess their own learning growth. Posting the learning target where students can clearly see it provides a continual reminder to them of where they are going. When students know where they are going, they can assess what they have mastered and what they have yet to learn.

How to Write a C U KAN

Figure 6.2 shows a sample of the *Concept*, *Understand*, *Know*, *Able to do* (skills), and *Now you get it!* components for several different content areas.

C U KAN Sample

The following is an example of a six-day lesson plan developed using the C U KAN model. C U KAN lessons can be longer projects, like the example, but they can also be short one-day lessons, homework, or even ongoing class work. Students can also work in groups or independently. Each component was written based on the "Learning Target" (Figure 6.3), which also appears at the beginning of the student handout for them to have as a reference and reminder of the learning target.

Rubrics for Student Assessment

Once you have developed a lesson using the C U KAN framework, you can easily develop the rubric for assessing how well students have mastered new knowledge, deepened their understanding, or developed

Figure 6.2   C U KAN Sample Learning Targets

	Social Studies	*Science*	*Math*	*Language Arts*
Concept The big idea of a unit/lesson, usually one word	Systems	Systems	Number sense	Purpose
Understand that The underlying principle that connects the content to students' lives	Understand that a democratic government maintains a system of checks and balances so that no one way of thinking can take over.	Understand that a decrease in habitat contributes to a decrease in the population of local species.	Understand that everything is made up of wholes and parts.	Understand that writers use persuasive techniques to convince others of a point of view.
Know The key facts and key vocabulary words that support the understandings	Fascism Hitler Goering Allies Major events and dates that led to WWII	Contributing factors to habitat destruction Habitat conversion Predation Endangerment	Numerator Denominator Equivalent fractions	Types of persuasive communication techniques
Able to Do The basic skills, social skills, production skills, and/or skills of the discipline students will be able to do to work toward the understandings	Read and comprehend text Note taking Group work	Research via field study or online investigation Comprehend text Gather data Interpret data	Compare whole numbers and fractions Multiplication Division Work independently	Brainstorming Rough drafts Revision and editing techniques Make a goal and create a plan to follow through
Now You Get It! How students demonstrate their understanding of the above learning objectives	RAFT Plus: Role play from the perspective of a historical figure we studied	Choice Menu: Letter to the editor Data display with conclusions Public service announcement Children's book	Tiered Lesson: a. Create fraction strips at varying levels of complexity b. Create story problems from your life that show understanding of wholes and parts	Interest-Based Groups: Analyze writing models, then write a persuasive piece

Figure 6.3 Example of a Clear Learning Target

Learning Target	
Name: Kathleen Kryza	Grade Level of Lesson: High School

Concept (Overarching Theme): Inspirational Leadership
As a result, students should . . .

Understand That (Key principles)

- You can help to create Martin Luther King's dream by creating peace in yourselves, your community, and your world.
- Personal and outside influences shape people's cultural, religious, gender, and social beliefs.

Know (Facts)

- Peace, Freedom, Equal Rights, Fair, Nonviolence, Tolerance, Prejudice, Racism, Diversity (You decide which terms you wish students to comprehend.)
- MLK key principles for nonviolent protest

Able to Do (Skills/Be able to . . .)
Determine important from interesting facts about Dr. King and take effective notes for your project

their learning skills. Below are steps and suggestions for developing a rubric aligned to your C U KAN outline.

- The first two sections of the rubric are simply the *Understand* and *Know* of your C U KAN. And guess what? You already developed those at the beginning of your unit. Under the "Expectations" column of the rubric, add the *Understand* and *Know* objectives that you developed.
- The third section of the rubric is titled "Quality Work." Prior to starting to work on their projects, students are expected to develop at least three quality criteria specific to their project type, that is, skit, poster, and so on. The students must be specific and avoid using generic phrases such as, "We'll work hard," "We'll take our time," or "It will look good." (See the "Resources" section for ideas about quality project standards.)
- Before the students work on their projects, review their criteria for quality work. Students are not allowed to work on their project until you have initialed the rubric showing your approval of their criteria. This is important because when you are grading the quality section, the students will be graded based on the quality criteria that they committed to achieving on the project. (e.g., "You said you were going to have costumes and props in your skit, but you don't. That brings your grade down for that section of the rubric.")
- You might want to include sections on the rubric that assess learning skills, such as work habits, group effort, or note taking.

Figure 6.4 Example of a Planning Guide

Planning Guide
Preassess: How will you determine students' readiness, interests, or learning profiles before starting your lesson/unit? • Give content-specific interest survey regarding the civil rights movement and MLK • Use data from learning profile information gathered at the beginning of the year (Use the information from the preassessment to help design choices for the menu)
Prime: How will you engage the learners at the beginning of the lesson/unit? Show a video clip of MLK's "I Have a Dream" speech. Question students about his message, about what they think has changed since then, and about what needs to happen today to carry on the dream.
Where will you be differentiating instruction? Explain how you are differentiating as you describe that section of your lesson. • ☐ Chunk/Information Acquired • ☐ Chew/Information Processed • ☑ Check/Information Out • ☐ Content/The Information Will you be using a dynamic design for differentiating instruction? If so, which design: ☐ RAFT Plus   ☑ **Choice Designs**   ☐ Tiered   ☐ Contract   ☐ Compacting   ☐ Centers
Chunk: How will students acquire the new learning? Students will gather information from several sources, including books, the Internet, videos, etc.
Chew: How will students get to process the new learning? Students will be using the 1/3, 2/3 note-taking method to gather important information for their presentation. Students will meet to discuss information they are gathering at checkpoints within the research.
Check (ongoing assessment): How will you and/or students assess during the learning? Students will reflect with others on what they are learning and how it applies to the "understand" and "know" components of this unit.
NOW YOU GET IT! / Check for understanding: How will students show transfer of learning? • Notes will be collected • Students will demonstrate understanding by choosing a project from a choice menu. Students will self-assess on a rubric and then the teacher will give the final grade on the rubric.
The Information: (Materials, Books, Web sites, etc.) • Martin Luther King: Historical Perspective (DVD) ~ Martin Luther King • Biography—*Martin Luther King Jr.: The Man and the Dream* (A&E DVD Archives) DVD ~ Martin Luther King • The Greatest Speeches of All Time (DVD) ~ "I Have a Dream" speech by Martin Luther King • Citizen King (DVD) ~ Martin Luther King • Selected biographies of Martin Luther King • King Center Web Site: www.thekingcenter.com/ • Martin Luther King, Jr. Day On the Net: www.holidays.net/mlk/
Reflections: What worked? What would I do differently next time? More management tips and reminders I would have gathered more sources in advance and asked the media specialist to prepare the computers with the sites that my office assistant and I looked up. Students loved the project and learned so much. It was exciting to see them so engaged in history.

Figure 6.5   Example of Student Handout and Learning Target

Martin Luther King, Jr., Day

Choice Menu

Concept: Inspirational Leadership

Understand that:

- You can help to create MLK's dream by creating peace in yourselves, your community, and your world
- Personal and outside influences shape people's cultural, religious, gender, and social beliefs

Know:

- Peace, Freedom, Equal Rights, Fairness, Nonviolence, Tolerance, Prejudice, Racism, Diversity
- MLK key principles for nonviolent protest

Able to Do:

- Determine important from interesting facts about Dr. King
- Take effective notes for your project

Now You Get It!:

Choose one of the activities below to show what you understand and know about MLK's inspirational leadership.

Figure 6.6   Example of Student Handout

Create a skit or video public service announcement that talks to teens about today's prejudices and offers solutions based on Dr. King's philosophy.	Create a dialogue between Gandhi and King talking about a future world of peace and how it will be created. (Can be done in writing, skit, video, your choice)
Create a timeline of the major events of the American Civil Rights Movement from 1948 through today. (Create and include dates and actions that you imagine will occur in the future, as Dr. King's dream is being reached.)	Think deeply about one of Dr. King's beliefs (Peace, Freedom, Nonviolence, Equality) and create your choice of project to show your understanding. • Art • Writing • Music • Dance • Video • PowerPoint • Statistical Research •Scientific Data
Take Action! Create and follow through on a plan for helping Dr. King's dream in your school, town, state, or country.	Write a song/poem/rap to honor the life and achievements of Dr. Martin Luther King, Jr. You may present or record your presentation
Your choice (Must be given the okay by your teacher)	Research and present, write about, or make a brochure to illustrate the continuing work done by "The Martin Luther King Center for Nonviolent Social Change."

There could be a section for any of the *Able to do* skills that you developed under that "Able to do" in your C U KAN.

- After students have shared their projects, have them self-assess on the rubric by placing check marks in the boxes according to how they think they have performed. (To keep things simple, avoid having them assign themselves points.) They complete the self-assessment by giving themselves a grade and responding to these prompts: "What I/we did that was quality work . . ." and "What I/we could do better next time . . ." Then they turn in the rubric.
- Now, you fill out the same rubric only you put in the points. You add your grade and comments and return the rubrics to the students.

Using the Rubric With Students

- Students should receive the rubric as they begin to work on their projects. You can give students a copy of the rubric, show it to them on the overhead, or make a wall chart of it. Explain what's expected of them as you walk through the rubric.
- Connect self-assessment in school to the type of reflective self-assessing they will need to do as they enter the work world. Explain to students that they need to do quality work and be able to know when they are doing quality work. As they get better at self-assessing, they should find the scores they give themselves on the rubric become very close to the teacher's scores.
- Explain to students that the grade you give is the final grade because you are the professional, coach, and guide for their learning. You know what it looks like when they "get it."

C U KAN: Teaching Tips for All Lesson Designs

Included below are tips to keep in mind when you design any type of lesson using the C U KAN framework. At the ends of Chapters 7 through 12, there will be specific teaching tips for each of the six particular designs described in those chapters.

Lesson Design

- Develop the C U KAN for the lesson prior to designing the choices for students.
- All lesson designs can be short-term (lite-n-lean) or long-term (deep and dynamic) assignments. (For example, the lessons

Figure 6.7   Example of Rubric

Name(s): _____   _____

Project Choice: _____

Expectations	Excellent	Good	Okay	Needs Improvement
Shows knowledge of King's key principals for social justice _____ points				
Shows understanding of today's prejudices, MLK's dream, how it is your responsibility to help create the dream _____ points				
Quality work (as defined by you) _____ points				
Notes				

Three ways I/we will do quality work for this project: _____

_____

_____

_____

What I/we did that was quality work . . .

_____

What I/we could do better next time . . .

_____

Teacher Comments:

could take two days or two weeks and could consist of home-work or class work.)

- Lessons can be done alone or in groups.

Management Level

- Develop routines and procedures for things such as how to get materials, move around the room, control the noise level, clean up, and work in groups. Practice these procedures until students have them down. If students start to slack off on procedures, kindly have them practice them again.
- Assign students to make sure that the room is tidy and materials are put back where they are supposed to be.
- Students must do quality work on their product choice. Once students have picked their project type and have begun working on it, give them the assessment rubric. Note that quality work is one of the expectations on the rubric. At the bottom of the rubric, have students write down at least three criteria that tell *specifically* how they will do quality work for that project type.

For example, quality skit criteria could include the following:

1. We will use costumes.

2. We will know our parts.

3. We will rehearse at least three times.

- Have students develop a plan to show you what they are going to do. If they are working in groups, they must show that they have divided up the tasks so that everyone has a job to do.
- If students will be presenting their projects (skits, songs, etc.), make an advance sign-up sheet for students who need to present. Be very specific on how much presentation time will be allowed. (Usually, if students ramble on and use too much time, it's because they are not prepared.)
- If you're doing a long-term project, have students become "experts" before they work on the creative part of the project. This is a good time to model and scaffold how to do the vital know-how skills like note taking or using graphic organizers. Once they show you that they have the content knowledge, they can work on the project.
- While students are working on lessons, be sure to float around the room and check to see that they have the *Understand*, *Know*, and *Able to do* components in their projects.

Assessment Level

- The rubric should contain learning outcomes from the C U KAN. You can focus on the *Understand*, *Know,* and *Able to do* outcomes, as well as assessing quality work or group work. You can choose one area to focus on for assessment or a combination of areas. (See examples in lesson design chapters.)
- Always have students assess themselves on their projects first. Then you assess using the same rubric.
- You can use your C U KAN framework to preassess students prior to beginning a unit. For example, turn your C U KAN objectives into questions and have students write and/or draw what they know about the questions prior to starting the unit. Collect the information and use it to determine what students know and don't know about your topic.
- You can also have students self-assess during the learning process using the C U KAN objectives. For example, in the middle of a lesson or unit, you can ask students to give you a "thumbs up" if they get the objectives, a "thumbs sideways" if they somewhat get them, or a "thumbs down" if they are still confused. Having students self-reflect on the learning target helps them build ownership and responsibility for learning.
- If you are using a rubric to assess, have students assess themselves on the rubric. The goal is for them to be as close to the grade you would give them as possible. (You're the "boss," so your grade counts.)
- **Teacher Self-Assessment:** As you try out new dynamic designs, note what's working and what is not. Keep doing what *is* working, and troubleshoot what's not working.

Assessing Group Projects

- Assign students to groups according to choice, readiness, or learning profile. (If you assign groups by readiness, you can easily tier the assignment.)
- Have the students choose their jobs in the group. (Some jobs might be leader, scribe, teacher getter, organizer, timekeeper, and life coach.) Be sure to have the students be responsible for their jobs.
- As a class, discuss appropriate group behaviors. Design a group behavior rubric based on these discussions.
- Talk about the consequences of not working with the group. (If a person chooses to hurt and not help the group, he or she can be "fired" from the group and have to work on an independent activity.)

- Have the groups self-assess at the end of each work session. Then you, as their "boss," agree or disagree with their assessments.

How C U KAN Will Help You Differentiate

The C U KAN framework helps you differentiate because it gives you a clear map of what you want your students to understand, know, and be able to demonstrate. C U KAN also helps you design an aligned rubric that focuses on the essential learning points. You know what you are looking for and what it looks like when students get there.

C U KAN gives you the road map to begin differentiating:

1. How students take in the C U KAN information (*Chunk*)

2. How students process the C U KAN information (*Chew*)

3. How students demonstrate their understanding of the C U KAN (*Check*)

We can readily convey the importance of content to our students when we have a clear learning target to aim toward and when we make connections between that target and students' lives. Sharing the learning target encourages students to take responsibility for their own learning. They are able to self-reflect; they know when they are getting or not getting the targeted objectives. Starting with a clear learning target also allows us to think of alternative options for assessing and reporting students' progress toward learning outcomes. See, you *can* reach all types of learners and your learning target too. Once you have developed a C U KAN framework, integrating inspiring teaching and assessment is straightforward. See, you *can* easily design deep and dynamic lessons and rubrics for assessment. It's a cinch! So create your C U KAN, try out the following lesson designs, and have fun!

Deep and Dynamic Lesson Designs

Once you have developed the C U KAN framework for a lesson, you can decide which deep and dynamic design (Figure 6.8) will have the most benefit for the learning outcomes.

Figure 6.8   Deep and Dynamic Designs and the Benefits of Each

Deep and Dynamic Designs	Benefits
#1: Choice Menus	Engage students based on interests and learning profile Teach students to make choices Use for a variety of purposes (homework, class work, tests)
#2: RAFT Plus	Engage through students' interests and learning profiles Teach students to think from other perspectives Great for group projects
#3: Tiered Lessons	Engage students based on their readiness level Teach students to be realistic about when they are ready to learn new content Students challenged at appropriate readiness level
#4: Contracts	Engage students through learning profile, interests, and/or readiness level Teach students accountability Promote independent learning
#5: Learning Stations	Engage students through learning profile, interests, and/or readiness levels Teach students responsibility Can be exploratory or structured
#6: Compacting	Engage advanced learners Teach advanced learners to take risks Independent learning for advanced students

Looking Ahead to Deep and Dynamic Designs

In Chapters 7–12, we will explain each of the deep and dynamic designs by showing you the following:

1. A Teacher's Overview

This overview provides an introduction to each deep and dynamic design, so you can see the big picture of that design including the following:

- Why this design is important for today's students
- The knowledge you will need in order to design this lesson
- The skills you will acquire as a teacher

2. A Reoccurring Sample Learning Target for Each Design

See Resource G.1 for an example of a learning target—our sample concerns ecosystems—written according to each deep and dynamic design. There will also be a sample planning guide for implementing the design.

3. Content Area Examples

Each content example will have a key to help you easily find your way through the lessons.

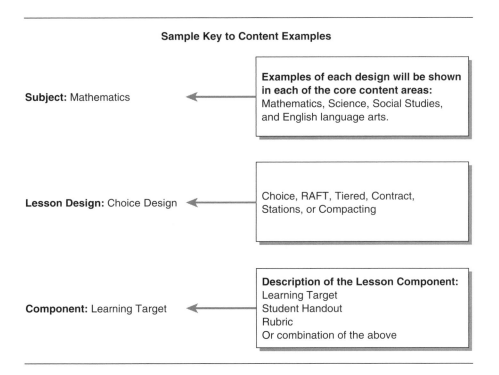

Sample Key to Content Examples

Subject: Mathematics

Examples of each design will be shown in each of the core content areas: Mathematics, Science, Social Studies, and English language arts.

Lesson Design: Choice Design

Choice, RAFT, Tiered, Contract, Stations, or Compacting

Component: Learning Target

Description of the Lesson Component: Learning Target Student Handout Rubric Or combination of the above

4. Teaching Tips

At the end of each chapter on lesson design, you will find teaching tips specific to helping you design, manage, and assess using that design.

Let's get started with our first design . . . Choice Designs!

7

Deep and Dynamic Design #1

Choice Menus

Teacher Overview

Concept: Choice menus are about exactly that, the power of "Choice."

Understand That (Key principles)

- Learners feel more in control of their learning environment and are more engaged, accountable, and responsible when they are given a voice and a choice in their learning.
- Learners must be taught how to make appropriate choices, how to follow through on their plans, and how to assess their progress.

Know (Facts)

Choice menus provide a graphic "menu" of activities from which students can select to show how they have learned the objectives of a lesson (C U KAN) or to reinforce the learning of a concept. Menus can be based on students' readiness, interests, or learning profiles. Choice options can take many forms; for example, in this chapter, you will learn about activity menus, dicing, tic-tac-toes, and cubing.

Able to Do (Skills/Be able to . . .)

- The teacher determines the C U KAN that students must know from a unit of study.
- The teacher creates a graphic menu or list of options for demonstrating what students must show they've learned (three to nine options on average).
- Menu options can be created according to students' readiness levels, interests, or learning profiles.
- Students choose their menu options and record their choices.
- Rubrics may be designed to facilitate student self-assessment or assessment by the teacher.

Now You Get It!

Choice designs will:
- Promote appropriate challenges for all learners
- Provide opportunities for success for all students
- Provide respectful and relevant learning activities for all students
- Allow for students to be more actively engaged in their learning process
- Promote students' responsibility, independence, and accountability
- Result in education that is highly engaging for students and teachers

Content Examples

Subject: Mathematics

Design: Choice

Lesson Component: Learning Target & Student Handout

Three-Dimensional Shapes Activity Menu

Understand That:

- Mathematicians develop common criteria for defining geometric shapes so that they can communicate

Know:

- Terms: Three-dimensional figure, face, prism, base, edge, cube, vertex/vertices, pyramid, cylinder, cone, sphere, net
- We find three-dimensional shapes in our everyday world.
- Length × Width × Height

Able to Do: Identify and create various three-dimensional shapes.

Now You Get It: Choose one activity from each row to help you to know and understand three-dimensional shapes.

Create a crossword puzzle and answer key using all the vocabulary terms	Draw pictures that represent all the vocabulary terms, or create a children's book that teaches about the terms	Do a skit that acts out the different vocabulary terms
Using two of the net patterns available, color, create, and form a 3-D shape. Be able to tell what your shape is and why it's named what it is.	Create and color your own net pattern, and put it together	Using a net design, create a 3-D model of something that could be seen in the world now or in the future
Do pages 410–411 Odd numbers	Do pages 410–411 Even numbers	Create your own math worksheet on 3-D shapes, and create an answer key to go with it

Lesson Component: Rubric

Three-Dimensional Shapes Project Rubric

How I Did	Great!	Good	Okay	Needs More Work
Understand that mathematicians develop common criteria for defining geometric shapes 5 points				
Know . . . Know 3-D shapes and $L \times W \times H$ Examples of 3-D shapes in our world 5 points				
Math Book Pages 5 points				
Work Habits Used time wisely Organized 5 points				

Subject: Science

Design: *Choice*

Lesson Component: *Learning Target & Student Handout*

Amphibians Choice Menu

Name _____   Student #_____

Concept: Systems

Understand That: An organism's external physical features enable it to carry out life functions in its particular environment

Know: Characteristics specific to amphibians; differences between amphibian species

PART 1: **Choices for** *learning*

For two class periods (11/7 & 11/8) choose a way to learn the basic facts of pages 76–83:

___ Work with teacher   ___ Work with a small group   ___ Work alone

PARTS 2 & 3: **Choices for reviewing and for assessment**

You will have three class periods (11/9, 11/14, and 11/15) to complete the following tasks. You may also work at home as needed.

1. Due Tuesday, Nov. 15th

2. Do one of the ten items below as review work

3. Due Wednesday, Nov. 16th

4. Do one of the ten items to present to the class for your assessment grade

Advice: You might want the one you present to the class for your assessment grade to be the cooler one of your two projects. Make sure you rehearse, so you are certain you are loud enough, slow enough, and interesting enough.

Amphibians Project Menu

Writing	Creating	Drawing/Building
__ Write a letter to a friend describing the characteristics of amphibians.	__ Create a rap teaching the characteristics of amphibians.	__ Build a model of an amphibian. Attach a list of its characteristics.
__ Compare the characteristics of two different kinds of amphibians (T-chart, Venn diagram, or plain lists).	__ Create a crossword puzzle using amphibian terms and their definitions.	__ Draw a poster of an imaginary amphibian. Label the characteristics that prove it is an amphibian.
__ Research one amphibian, and write a report about it and its characteristics.	__ Create a game that teaches or reviews facts about amphibians.	__ Design and make a poster that teaches the features of frogs/toads and of salamanders/newts.

OR ___ Develop your own unique way to show what you know and understand about amphibians. (Discuss your idea with the teacher *before you start.*)

Subject: Social Studies

Design: *Choice*

Lesson Component: *Learning Target & Student Handout*

Cultural Perspectives

Concept: Culture

As a result you should . . .

Understand That:

- A variety of cultural traits produce a variety of distinct cultural perspectives.
- Examination of the similarities and differences of different cultures strengthens the fabric of a multicultural society.

Know:

- Culture
- Cultural Traits
- Cultural Geography
- Cultural Convergence
- Cultural Diffusion
- Cultural Health

Able to Do:

- Identify cultural traits of your own and others' cultures
- Take notes
- Give effective oral presentation

Directions: Prepare an oral presentation sharing your creations with the class. The presentation must include the essential ideas above and your examination of how similarities and differences between different cultures strengthen the fabric of a multicultural society.

Please choose two of the following four options to explain your own culture:

- – writing a one-page summary
- – drawing a picture
- – composing a song or poem
- – writing a skit

NOTE: Created by Mike Huff, Michigan Teacher

Lesson Component: Rubric

Cultural Perspectives

Expectations	Super!	Sufficient	So-So	Slipped
Understand that . . . • A variety of cultural traits produces a variety of distinct cultural perspectives • Examination of how the similarities and differences of different cultures strengthen the fabric of a multicultural society. 20 Points	• Shows complex understanding of the concepts; • Supports with data from text; • Explores related ideas _____ Points	• Understands the concepts; • Uses some text references; • Explores ideas beyond facts and details _____ Points	• Limited understanding of key concepts; • Limited text reference; • Little depth or elaboration of idea _____ Points	• Little understanding of the concept; • No or inaccurate reference to text _____ Points
Know • Key facts and information about your culture 20 Points	• Precise facts; • In depth and well supported _____ Points	• Covers facts effectively; • Well developed _____ Points	• Valid facts but little depth or elaboration _____ Points	• Needs more facts; • Needs accurate facts _____ Points
Quality Work • As defined by you (see below) 10 Points	• Unique, fresh or imaginative work _____ Points	• Creatively integrates work _____ Points	• Met quality work criteria _____ Points	• Does not meet quality work criteria _____ Points
• Oral Presentation 10 Points	_____ Points	_____ Points	_____ Points	_____ Points

Three ways I/we will do quality work for our project: _____

_____

_____

_____

_____

_____

Teacher Initials: _____
What I/we did that was quality work:

_____

_____

_____

_____

_____

What I/we could do better next time:

Student Grade: _____   Teacher Grade: _____

Subject: English Language Arts

Design*: Choice*

Lesson Component: *Learning Target & Student Handout*

Comprehension Skills Choice Menu

Understand That: Good readers have various strategies they use to comprehend text.

Know: The events and key people from your chapter

Able to Do: Apply comprehension strategies to help you complete one of the tasks below:

Comprehension #1 Analyze the author's motives for including this chapter in the book.	*Comprehension #2* Write a brief summary of the main events in the chapter from the perspective of one of the characters. Now write another summary of the events from another character's perspective.
Comprehension #3 Illustrate two pivotal scenes that show your understanding of the key events in the chapter.	*Comprehension #4* Develop six questions related to this chapter, one at each level of Bloom's taxonomy. Create an answer key to go with your questions.
Comprehension #5 Create a rap/poem/song by restating the main problem in the chapter. What was the cause of the problem? What was the solution? Be sure to give details.	*Comprehension #6* Evaluate what you think the main character might do next. Explain why, verbally or in writing, citing examples from the book.

SOURCE: Adapted from Cathy Schneider, Whitmore Lake Schools.

Choice Design: Teaching Tips

Lesson Design

- When starting, try with fewer choices. Keep it simple for your own benefit.
- It helps to give students some examples of what you want them to do. (If you spell out everything for students, then they don't learn how to develop the skills on their own). If you don't have past student examples to share, try coming up with some simple examples yourself.
- Students can be expected to do only one choice or several choices on the menu, depending on the time you have and the complexity of the choices.
- Have one of the choices on the menu be "Your Choice: Must be approved by Teacher." Why? Students will come up with amazing ideas when you open the door for them to do so.
- If you include a choice on your menu that's traditional, for example, "Do page 23 in the book," and most students choose that, next time you do a menu don't include that choice. If you still want something traditional, but you want to challenge them, have the choice be, "Design a worksheet/test and make an answer key to go along with it."

Management

- Students must do quality work on their product choice. Prior to working on their product, students must write down at least three criteria to tell you specifically how they will do quality work for that project type. (Quality Skit Criteria: We will use costumes, know our parts, and rehearse at least three times.) You will be grading them on the three criteria they identified, so you want these to be really specific. See the "Resources" section for more specifics on quality work.
- Collecting Work
  - Number the menu choices and collect by number. (All those who did #1, please turn in your posters at this time, etc.),
  - If students will be presenting their projects (skits, songs, etc.), make an advance sign-up sheet for students who need to present. Be very specific about how much presentation time will be allowed. (Usually, if students ramble on and use too much time, it's because they are not prepared.)

Assessment

- Correct by project type. Correct all the posters, then all the poems, and so on. This gets you in the "groove" of the project type.
- Design rubrics that allow for grading different project types with the same rubric. See the rubric examples in this section.
- Remember that when you first start giving kids choices, some will do an amazing job, and some will slop through it. It's a good idea, the first few times you try a menu, to share several products of students who have done quality work so the class begins to understand what you are expecting. The more you expect and show them how to reach quality in their work, the more you will begin to see it! (Start keeping examples of quality projects that students have completed so that you can share them as examples in future classes).
- You can assign different levels of points for different options on a menu and have students choose what grade level option they are working for on their project (A, B, or C), or every menu option can be worth the same point value.
- **Teacher Self-Assessment**: If students are doing great projects, but they are still missing the target, you might need to investigate the clarity of your stated learning objectives. Check that your C U KAN is written right on the menu and that you keep reminding students to refer back to the outcomes to ensure they are demonstrating correct and thorough understanding.

8

Deep and Dynamic Design #2

RAFT Plus

Teacher Overview

Concept: Perspective

Understand That (Key principles)

Students gain deeper understandings about content if they engage from the perspective of something or someone within that content.

Know (Facts)

The RAFT format

R = Role (can be animate or inanimate)

A = Audience (someone or something affected by or connected to the role)

F = Format (choices based on learning styles or multiple intelligences)

T = Task/learning outcome (the *Understand*, *Know*, and *Able to do* of your objectives)

Able to Do (Skills/Be able to . . .)

- The teacher determines the outcomes that students must know from a unit of study.
- The teacher creates a few RAFT Plus options for demonstrating what students learn (three to five on average).
- RAFT Plus options can be tiered by choice, by interests, or by readiness level.
- Students work independently or in groups to create self-selected projects to show their understanding of concepts studied.
- Teacher and students use rubrics to assess completed products from the RAFT Plus projects.

Now You Get It!

RAFT Plus lessons will:
- Promote student initiative
- Provide opportunities for success for all students
- Provide learning opportunities that are relevant to students
- Allow for students to be more actively engaged in their learning process
- Promote students' responsibility, independence, and accountability
- Are fun to do!

Content Examples

Subject: Mathematics

Design: RAFT Plus

Lesson Component: Learning Target

Lesson Component: Student Handout & Rubric

Learning Target

Concept:

- As a result, students should . . .

Understand That:

- Mathematicians look for ways to work efficiently with large numbers

Know:

- Exponent
- Base number
- Rules for exponents

Able to Do: Add exponents, determine with base numbers

Now You Get It: Students will demonstrate understanding in a RAFT format from the point of view of an exponent.

RAFT Plus Assignment: Power to the Exponents!

Role	An exponent
Audience	Base number
Format	Skit, children's book, comic strip, song, your choice (see teacher)
Tasks	Explain what you do to the base number and how you help mathematicians; give an example; teach one of the rules for using exponents

Expectations	Awesome	Average	Adequate	Additional Effort Needed
Understand Exponents are a more efficient way to indicate that a number is multiplied by itself _____ Points				
Know Exponent Base number Rules for exponents _____ Points				
Quality Work _____ Points				
Used Time Wisely _____ Points				

Subject: Science

Design: RAFT Plus

Lesson Component: Learning Target & Student Handout

Stem Cells: Pro/Con—RAFT Assignment

Role	A person either for or against stem cell research
Audience	Society
Format	Skit/video (e.g., televised debate)
	Song/rap/poem
	Brochure
	Newspaper or magazine article
	Your choice (see teacher for okay)
Tasks	Research from your viewpoint and try to persuade society to adopt your viewpoint

---

Learning Target

Understand That: Scientific thinking grows through quality research and debate

Know: Key terms related to your research

Able to Do: Research and gather data. Use persuasive techniques to convince others to see your point of view.

Subject: Social Studies

Design: *RAFT Plus*

Lesson Component: *Learning Target & Student Handout*

RAFT Assignment: Marketplace

Role	Buyer or seller
Audience	Buyer or seller
Format	Skit

Tasks	*Buyers*	*Sellers*
	1. Determine your income level	1. Determine your product and price
	2. Determine what products you need	2. Create your products
	3. Bargain to get the best price	3. Bargain to get the most money

Concept: Culture

Understand That:

- Cultures develop their own economies based on their needs, wants, and resources.

Know:

- The Latin American marketplace and its economic purpose in the culture
- Terms: Bargaining and exchange

Able to Do: Create a graphic organizer that shows what you have learned about cultures and economy.

Now You Get It: Create a RAFT project that shows what you understand and know about world marketplaces.

Lesson Component: Rubric

RAFT Assignment: Marketplace Rubric

Expectations	So Super	So Okay	So-So	So. . . . Merits Further Effort
Understand That cultures develop their own economies based on their needs, wants and resources _____ Points				
Know • Marketplace and its purpose • Bargaining and exchange • Foreign currency _____ Points				
Used Time Wisely _____ Points				

Subject: English Language Arts

Design: *RAFT Plus*

Lesson Component: *Learning Target & Student Handout*

COURAGE: RAFT Plus Project

Role	A character from *Iron Will* or *White Fang*
Audience	Teenagers today

Format

Song/poem/rap	Comic strip
Children's book	Motivational speech
Advice column	Public service announcement

Task   Share what this character learned about courage, and give advice about how to be courageous in today's world

Concept: Courage

Learning Target

Understand That: People show courage in different ways, for different purposes, and under various circumstances.

Know: The attributes of courage demonstrated by the main character in your story

Able to Do: Read a story and make a story map showing how your character showed courage and under what circumstances.

Now You Get It: Create a project from the perspective of one of the characters that shows your understanding and knowledge of the concept of courage.

Lesson Component: *Rubric*

Courage Rubric

Expectations	Super	Sufficient	So-So	Slipped
Showed understanding of courage in the story and how that might look for teens today _____Points				
Described attributes of courage _____Points				
Quality work (As defined by you) _____ Points				
Used class time well _____ Points				

Three ways I/we will do quality work for our project:

_____

_____

What I/we did that was quality work . . .

What I/we could do better next time . . .

RAFT Plus: Teaching Tips

Lesson Design

- Note to beginners: When you first try a RAFT, it's okay to have all students work from the same information about role, audience, format, and task. As you evolve in your skills, you can begin giving them more options within the RAFT.
- Try to offer choices in the RAFT project. You can change the role and the format quite easily. You can assign different roles to different students or have different audiences. (For example, half the class could be colonists, the other half loyalists, and they could present to each other why they have chosen to be on that side.)

Management

- If students are working from different roles, have them move to different parts of the room. For example, have the colonists work in one half of the room and the loyalists in the other. This makes it easier for you to work with the different roles if you need to pull them together, and it also allows students working from the same perspective to collaborate more readily.

Assessment

- Remember that, when you first start giving kids RAFT Plus assignments, some will do an amazing job, and some will slop through it. It's a good idea, the first few times you try a RAFT Plus, to give demonstrations of quality work (e.g., model skits or effective debates) and to share several products of students who have done quality work (e.g., products such as letters, commercials, or recordings of performances). Then the class begins to understand what you are expecting. The more you expect and show them how to reach quality in their work, the more you will begin to see it!
- **Teacher Self-Assessment:** As you try out RAFT Plus, reflect on what's working and what is not working. For example, if students have found great content but aren't really stepping into the role, you may have to model a few examples of "becoming" someone or something else to help them see what you are expecting.

9

Deep and Dynamic Design #3

Tiered Lessons

Teacher Overview

Concept: Readiness

Understand That (Key principles)

- Learners must have a challenge that is appropriate for them in order for learning to occur.
- Students experience more success when learning occurs at the level of challenge that is appropriate for them.

Know (Facts)

- In a mixed ability classroom, the teacher develops levels of lessons based on the same curriculum concept (essential idea) so that students may experience the learning at their appropriate ability level.

Able to Do (Skills/Be able to . . .)

- The teacher determines the basic concepts that students must understand, know, and do from a unit of study.
- The teacher preassesses to find the background knowledge of students for that unit of study.
- Based on the preassessment, the teacher decides how many tiers of learning need to be developed.
- The teacher develops meaningful and respectful tasks for each tier of learners to accomplish.
- The teacher plans anchor activities for students to work on if the teacher is explaining to other groups or if students finish work early.
- The teacher develops authentic assessment tools to assess student learning at all tiers

Now You Get It!

Tiered lessons will:
- Promote appropriate challenge for all learners
- Provide opportunities for success for all students
- Provide respectful and relevant learning activities for all students
- Allow for students to be more actively engaged in their learning process
- Promote students' responsibility, independence, and accountability

Content Examples

Subject: Mathematics

Design: *Tiered Lessons*

Lesson Component: *Learning Target & Student Handout*

Destination Dice! Proportions

You will be working in groups of three to complete six activities that will help you gain a deeper understanding of our learning target.

Understand That:

- Mathematicians use numerical comparisons to solve for unknowns.

Know:

- Terms: Means and extremes, product, variable
- Product of the means = Product of the extremes

Able to Do:

- Solve for a variable.
- Find a product.
- Collaborate for clear understanding of objectives.

Now You Get It:

The "Destination Dice" handout you received is unique for your group's readiness level. Each card on the handout corresponds to the numbers on a die. Take turns rolling the die to determine your destiny. The activity that corresponds with the number you roll will be the activity you are responsible for (two each). Roll until all six activities are assigned. Work on your assigned cards, asking for guidance from your teammates when necessary. Once all six cards are complete, take turns reflecting on the activity, where it brought you in your understanding, and checking with your partners to see that they understand it too. No one understands until we all understand!

Destination Dice: Sheet 1

Diagram how to solve for **x**:

$$\frac{14}{x} = \frac{8}{20}$$

Extract a proportion from the word problem:

If 12 inches corresponds to 30.28 centimeters, how many centimeters are there in 15 inches?

Change one "extreme" on Card 1 and solve it again using a diagram.

Explain in a short paragraph how and which extreme you changed and what happened to the variable as a result.

Create a humorous word problem that is modeled by

$$\frac{3\,ft}{17\,lbs} = \frac{1.8\,ft}{x}$$

Describe how proportions can be used in cooking.

Destination Dice: Sheet 2

Diagram how to solve for x:

$$\frac{3}{45} = \frac{1}{5x}$$

Extract a proportion from the word problem:
The tax on a property with an assessed value of $360,000 is $2,450. What is the assessed value of a house whose family pays $5,200 in property taxes?

Change one "extreme" on Card 1 and solve it again using a diagram.

Explain in a short paragraph how and which extreme you changed and what happened to the variable as a result.

Create a humorous word problem that is modeled by

$$\frac{3" \text{ tall}}{8.5" \text{ wide}} = \frac{x}{2 \text{ ft wide}}$$

Describe how proportions can be used in architecture.

Destination Dice: Sheet 3

Diagram how to solve for x:

$$\frac{(2x + 1)}{2} = \frac{(x + 2)}{5}$$

Extract a proportion from the word problem: I want to lay a paver brick patio that will extend 15 ft. from my house. A professional landscaper recommends a ¼" drop for every 4 ft. length of patio so water will run off. How much lower should the end of my patio be?

Change one "extreme" on Card 1 and solve it again using a diagram.

Explain in a short paragraph how and which extreme you changed and what happened to the variable as a result.

Create a humorous word problem that is modeled by

$$\frac{4 \text{ marked}}{72 \text{ total}} = \frac{96 \text{ marked}}{x}$$

Describe how proportions can be used in biological research.

Subject: Science

Design: Tiered Lessons

Lesson Component: Learning Target & Student Handout

Choose Your Challenge: Space Exploration

With this mission, if you choose to accept it, you will . . .

Understand That:

- Technological advances allow us to discover more about our universe.
- Space exploration impacts our daily lives, positively and negatively.

Know:

- Six ways of exploring space: space station, space shuttle, rocket, space probe, satellite, telescope
- Pros and cons of each means of exploration
- Financial implications of space discovery
- Spin-offs and scientific advancements related to the space program

Able to Do:

- Research scientific discoveries in space.
- Collaborate with a group when choosing and completing activities.

Mission: *The Space Exploration Tool (from here on called "SET") that your team will research is (circle the one assigned to your team):*

space station   space shuttle   rocket   space probe   satellite   telescope

Captain's Orders: *This is a long-term project (about one week). Prepare ahead, plan well, and work as a TEAM, and you will be successful. Use the resources suggested but also explore other resources yourself. This project replaces book work. Treat it with curiosity, exploration, excitement, and responsibility. The teacher reserves the right to abandon the mission if the crew members are not reaching their goals!!!*

Procedure:

- Establish the following roles in your group:

Captain: keeps the crew on task, guides the crew when members are unsure of the next action to take

Engineer: keeps the mission log updated by filling it out daily

Technician: supplies the crew with necessary equipment to do activities; gathers and returns supplies

Scientist: keeps up with the data that the crew collects such as copies of Internet resources, books, magazines, and so on.

- Make a preliminary list of the topics you want to research.
- From the lists below, choose the activities that will best help your team reach the learning target. Each activity should be specific to the SET that was assigned to you. You can choose from challenge, super challenge, or mega challenge categories. The goal is to earn your crew 100 points. You can combine activities from any level of challenge to reach this value.
- Your book would be a great tool as a starting point for gathering information about your mission.
- Fill out your mission log so that each crew member has a job to do and knows when to do it. I suggest a small job each day for each crew member.
- You will summarize your discoveries about your SET with a three- to four-minute presentation. Use your rubric as a guideline for preparing your presentation.

Mission Termination Date: _____

Challenge Activities:

- Create a timeline of scientific progress for your project. (15 points)
- Read 18:8. Write a short paragraph or create a concept map discussing the pros and cons of the space program. (10 points)
- List the addresses of five Web sites that have information about your SET. (5 points)
- Create a movie poster advertising a new movie about Wernher von Braun—include his picture and an exciting description of his life. (20 points)
- Write a report of important findings related to your SET in the past 20 years. (15 points)
- Answer the section review questions in the chapter (#1–#15) in complete sentences with thorough answers. (2 points each question)
- Draw a cartoon of your SET. Include your findings. (15 points)
- Keep a diary of a scientist who is slowly discovering things in space using your SET. (15 points)
- Develop five hand signals you could send to another person on a space walk that deal with safety issues important to both of you. (5 points)

Super Challenge Activities:

- Create a professional display of original pictures related to your SET, noting how it works and labeling its structural components. (30 points)
- Present a news report of recent findings related to your SET. (35 points)
- Perform a TV commercial advertising a product that is a spin-off of something used in your space program. (30 points)
- Design a biographical poster of three scientists who have made significant contributions to space exploration. (30 points)
- For space station SET only: Read through some excerpts of reports from the International Space Station and write journal entries as if you were a scientist on board. Discuss problems you may have with cosmonauts from other countries and the political pulls that keep the future of the ISS uncertain. (25 points)

Mega Challenge Activities:

- Create a three-dimensional model of your SET and label the parts. (45 points)
- Demonstrate for your colleagues how your SET works. (Use a model, draw on the board, use overheads, or do a PowerPoint presentation.) (45 points)
- Design a promotional video to get funding for your SET. This must include past successes and a picture or model of your set—really sell yourself and your project!!! (50 points)
- Stage a debate highlighting the pros and cons of the space program. Have facts to support your opinions. (40 points)

Mission Log

Crew Member	Role

Name of crew: _____

Space Exploration Tool (SET): _____

Topics/Ideas/Brainstorming: _____

_____

_____

_____

Book reference pages: _____

Information to Be Gathered	Crew Member Responsible	Date	How You Doin'? (1–5)

Lesson Component: Learning Target & Student Handout

Space Exploration Rubric

Expectations	To the Stars!	To the Moon!	Circling in Earth's Atmosphere	Grounded for Technical Difficulties
Understand ❑ Technology has shaped our view of the universe ❑ The daily impacts of space exploration on our lives 15 Points	❑ Shows complex understanding of concepts ❑ Supported by various research and sources	❑ Understands the concepts ❑ Supported with a few sources	❑ Limited understanding of concepts ❑ Supported with one source	❑ Little understanding of concept ❑ Supported by text only
Know ❑ Six means of exploration ❑ Pros and cons of space program (spin-offs, scientific advancements, financial concerns) 15 Points	❑ Accurate facts supported by numerous examples with excellent elaboration and debate	❑ Correct facts supported by a few examples with sound arguments for debate	❑ Valid facts with examples from limited sources and little support for debate	❑ Needs more facts supported with examples and accurate arguments
Choosing Your Challenge 10 Points	❑ Challenged yourself to higher orbits and deeper understandings	❑ Challenged yourself above your expectations	❑ Some challenging parts	❑ Little or no challenge evident
Quality Work as determined below 10 Points	❑ Considerable	❑ More than average	❑ Sufficient	❑ Minimal or none

Ways we will do quality work for our project:

1.
2.
3.

What quality work we are most proud of and why.

What we could do better next time.

Subject: Social Studies

Design: *Tiered RAFT Plus Lesson*

Lesson Component: *Learning Target & Student Handout*

A Different Point of View: RAFT Plus Assignment

Yellow Group

Role	Japanese Americans from time of WWII
Audience	Americans from today
Format	Skit/video, children's book, news exposé, song, newspaper article, letter to a family in Japan, your choice (see teacher for okay)
Tasks	Describe what it felt like to be placed in a settlement camp, and tell what life was like there.

Blue Group

Role	Arab Americans today
Audience	Non-Arab Americans from today
Format	Skit/video, panel discussion, news exposé, song, newspaper article or political cartoon, PowerPoint presentation, your choice (see teacher for okay)
Tasks	There's talk about placing Arab Americans in settlement camps. Use your knowledge of what happened to Japanese Americans in WWII to convince your neighbors that it is not a good idea to repeat history.

Green Group

Role	A senator or congressman/congresswoman
Audience	Your fellow representatives in Congress or the Senate and the president
Format	Skit/video, debate, editorial, PowerPoint presentation to Congress, letter, your choice (see teacher for okay)
Tasks	Can and should Congress curtail the rights of Americans of international background if we go to war with their country of ancestry.

Lesson Component: *Rubric*

Criteria for Grading	Super	Sufficient	So-So	Slipped
Understands that democratic governments need to exercise caution when making decisions about people's rights. _____ Points				
Know facts about interment camps _____ Points				
Quality work (As defined below) _____ Points				
Final presentation _____ Points				
Ways I/we will do quality work for our project: 1. _____ 2. _____ 3. _____				

TOTAL POINTS: Student: _____   Teacher: _____

What I/we did that was quality work . . .

_____

_____

What I/we could do better next time . . .

_____

_____

_____

NOTE: This lesson was created by Kathleen Kryza, Infinite Horizons.

Subject: English Language Arts

Design: Tiered Lessons

Lesson Component: Student Handout

> NOTE: Each tier group has a handout like the one below but related to the group's assigned story.

Papa's Parrot: Reading the Story

Before Reading:

Before reading the short story "Papa's Parrot," read and discuss the following on pages 478–479:

- Meet the author (Cynthia Rylant)
- Literature and You
- Literary Focus
- Reading Strategy (You don't have to do the chart unless you want to.)

Key Vocabulary: (All group members need to understand the meaning of these words)

resumed   inflammatory   rheumatism   solemn

During Reading (pages 480–483)

- As you read, think about the following:
- Who is telling the story?
- Who are the protagonist and antagonist of the story?
- What is the climax of the story?
- What is the resolution of the story?

After Reading (Remember: Good readers reread text!)
Discuss the "Critical Thinking, Interpret" section on page 483.

Lesson Component: C U KAN and Rubric

Learning Target

Understand That:

- Writers let us into their characters' minds so we can learn from the internal conflict the characters' experience.
- We can handle internal conflict in positive or negative ways.

Know:

- Key vocabulary for comprehending your story
- The plot outline and elements for your story
  - theme, internal conflict, inferences

Able to Do:

- Demonstrate ability to use different voices in written or oral communication.

Now You Get It: Create and present a RAFT Plus.

Short Story Rubric

NAMES:
Title of Story:

Criteria For Grading	WOW! Best Possible Effort	WELL DONE! Pretty Good Effort	WELL, OKAY. Average Effort	WHAT! Little or No Effort
Group Daily Effort 10 points				
Plot Outline (Know) (Introduction, Rising/Falling Action, Climax, Resolution, Internal Conflict, Theme) 10 Points				
Lesson Target Understands what the character learned Understands how conflict can be handled 15 Points				
Quality Work/ Final Presentation (As defined below) 15 Points				

Total Points: _____

Ways I/we will do quality work for our project: _____

_____

_____

_____

_____

_____

_____

What I/we did that was quality work . . .

_____

_____

_____

_____

_____

_____

What I/we could do better next time . . .

_____

_____

_____

_____

_____

_____

Tiered Lessons: Teaching Tips

Lesson Design

- Note to beginners: When you first try a tiered lesson, it's okay to have just two tiers. You could have most of your students doing one lesson and a small group, either your advanced or struggling learners, working on another tier. As you evolve in your skills, you may choose to have more than two tiers.
- You can tier classroom discussion questions, homework assignments, or tests. Any lesson can become a tiered lesson.
- Trust us on this one! It seems challenging to tier lessons when you first get started, but as you begin seeing how your students respond when they are working at their appropriate readiness level, your brain will start to think in tiers. It gets easier, especially if you start with your C U KAN target in mind.

Management

- Establishing the environment at the beginning of the year will help you manage the class as you begin doing tiered lessons. From day one, begin setting the classroom tone that "Fair is not everybody getting the same thing, fair is everybody getting what they need to be successful." Your class will be prepared and will more readily accept students' working at different levels in your classroom.
- Anchor activities are a must when doing tiered lessons. Students will be starting and finishing at different times, so you want to have a plan for what they are expected to do if they are waiting for you or if they finish early. (See the "Resources" section for anchor activity ideas.)
- As you know, advanced learners need more academic challenge. When you allow them to work together from time to time during the year, you give them the opportunity to challenge each other and go really deep in their thinking, thus preventing the boredom that can lead to management problems.
- Students with lower readiness levels are often grouped with students who will end up doing the work for them. Knowing that someone will always help them out or do the work for them can contribute to the learned helplessness characteristic of these students. When we group lower readiness level students together, a new leader often emerges. This grouping gives students the support they need and teaches them to grow and build their skills instead of relying on others.

- Because students are working in tiers at their appropriate readiness levels, you can float around the room giving students the appropriate support they need. For example, you can offer more challenge to the top group if you see they need more, and you can help the lower group break down the task into manageable chunks.

Assessment

- Preassessment is an important part of preparing to do a tiered lesson. You can preassess by giving a short pretest using journal prompts, exit cards, oral response, and so on. (See the "Resources" section for more detailed preassessing information.)
- If you are using a rubric, the rubric should have the "Understand," "Know," and "Quality Work" headings, and headings for whatever other category you may choose to assess. See the "Resources" section for information on creating rubrics. Even though students are working at different levels of depth and complexity, they should be working toward the same objectives.
- **Teacher Self-Assessment**: As you try out tiered lessons, reflect on what's working and what is not working. For example, if you find that students are all finishing at different times or that you need to get one tier started and need something for the other tiers to be working on, you need to plan anchor activities as a management technique.

10

Deep and Dynamic Design #4

Contracts

Teacher Overview

Concept: Commitment

Understand That (Key principles)

- Contracts help students see that they are responsible for their own learning.
- Students become self-reflective when we give them ownership of their learning.

Know (Facts)

- Teachers can design individual or class contracts.
- Contracts can be designed at different readiness levels.
- Contracts can address behavior as well as academics.

Able to Do (Skills/Be able to . . .)

- The teacher creates either individual or group contracts that have choices and guidelines.
- Students read and commit to the contract by signing it.
- Students are accountable for completing the terms of the contract.
- Students are given a timeline for completing the work agreed to in the contract.

Now You Get It!

Contracts will:
- Provide challenges and eliminates boredom
- Allow for student choice
- Develop student commitment and responsibility skills

Content Examples

Subject: Mathematics

Design: *Contract*

Lesson Component: *Learning Target & Student Handout*

Functions and Graphs Contract

I, _____, will demonstrate my understanding of the learning objective by _____.
                 (date)

_____

- I will remain focused on my work and will study on my own time as well as during school time.
- I will contact Mr. Ennis if at any point I believe I will be unable to complete this unit as agreed.
- I will be resourceful in finding answers and getting help:
  - I will ask at least two classmates before consulting the teacher.
  - I will use my book and notes to look up relevant information.
  - If necessary, I will make an appointment with Mr. Ennis to review information.

Contract Part A: Must do

Read examples 1–3 of sections 5.2 and 5.3 from the algebra text. Write your own examples, with different equations and graphs, similar to these examples.

Contract Part B: Pick any three activities from the list below

- Describe three everyday examples (in at least one page) of pairs of quantities that have a functional relationship. Invent values for each quantity, write an equation describing each relationship, and show each on a graph.
- Complete fifteen of the "Practice by Example" problems in each of the two sections.
- Complete practice sheets 5.2 and 5.3, all even numbers.
- Complete five of the "challenge" problems at the end of each section, with at least 80% accuracy.
- Write a reflection in PAX (two paragraphs) about what function equations show and how graphs depend on the equations.
- Complete ten of the "Apply Your Skills" problems in each of the two sections.

- Design a business in which you sell a product (counts as two activities).

  – Describe the product, the cost of producing it, and the price you will charge.
  – Describe start-up costs.
  – Create equations to describe your income and profit.
  – Graph these equations.
  – Write a one-page reflection on some of the considerations one must make when running a business. This should include unpredictable changes in expenses, how your model depends on the demand for your product, and why it is necessary to use equations to help you understand the operation of your business.

Student's Signature: _____

In studying the concept of relationships, your choices that you complete from above must show that you:

Understand That:

- Mathematicians develop rules that help them see relationships so they can apply mathematical concepts to the actual events and circumstances of our lives.

Know:

- Terms: Functional relationships, function rules, variables
- Relationship between functional relationships and functional rules

Able to Do:

- Write rules of a function for specific situations.
- Graph function rules.
- Solve an equation for variables.

SOURCE: This lesson was created by John Ennis, Waterford, Michigan.

Subject: Science

Design: Contract

Lesson Component: Learning Target & Student Handout

Am I Making Healthy Choices?

You will *document your eating habits* for a 48-hour period. You will *create a graph* of your dietary habits and *evaluate your eating habits* according to recommended nutritional expertise. Last, you will *make a dietary plan* that would improve your dietary choices. These activities will lead you to . . .

Understand That:

- Health maintenance is affected by our daily behaviors and choices.

Know:

- Food groups from the Food Guide Pyramid
- The daily recommended serving sizes for each food group
- Elements of a nutritional food label
- The effects of diet on health maintenance

Able to Do:

- Read a nutritional label.
- Keep an accurate record of your daily diet.
- Convert nutritional information into food groups and serving sizes.
- Analyze data, create a graph, and make conclusions about dietary choices.
- Use the Food Guide Pyramid to plan a healthy daily diet.

Working Guidelines

You will be granted the freedom to work in your own time and in your own learning style to demonstrate your understanding of the above learning targets.

- Work quietly and stay on task without disturbing other students. These expectations also apply when you are working in other locations beside the classroom.
- When you need help, please quietly ask another student who is working on the same activity.
- If the teacher is conferencing with another student, do not disturb unless it is an emergency.

- Review your work, and use the rubric to self-assess before you turn in your work.

I agree to the above conditions. If I do no follow the above conditions, I will lose this opportunity to use my time as freely and will work under the teacher's direction.

Student Signature: _____   Date: _____

SOURCE: This lesson was created by Tricia Morrissey, Waterford, Michigan.

Subject: Social Studies

Design: *Contract*

Lesson Component: *Learning Target & Student Handout*

Physical Features Contract

By signing this contract, I, _____, agree to follow the rules and procedures of the assignment. I understand that if I do not follow the rules and procedures, it will have a negative impact on my grade.

I agree to have the following projects _____ completed by _____.

1. I will always work to the best of my ability.

2. I will stay focused while working on my activities.

3. I will ask questions when I do not understand something.

4. I will find and use other resources than those provided.

5. I understand that I am responsible for all of my work at all times.

Teacher-Student Conference: You may sign up for a personal conference to check on your progress or ask any questions.

Check which option you choose.

_____ Yes, I Want a Conference on _____Date

_____ No, I Do Not Want a Conference

Teacher _____   Date _____

Student _____   Date _____

Lesson Component: Learning Target & Student Handout

You will demonstrate your understanding of the following learning objective:

Concept: Human and environment interaction

Understand That: Human systems and their characteristics, such as population density and economy, are affected by physical systems (the environment).

Know:

- Terms: Population density and economy
- Major mountain ranges, rivers, seas, and lakes
- Five geographical themes of social studies

Able to Do:

- Study maps of Europe.
- Take notes from a video, distinguishing important from interesting information.
- Synthesize ideas from group discussions.
- Analyze the five geographical themes as they relate to the interaction between Europe's physical features and its population and economy.

Part 1: Complete the following task before moving on to Part 2
   Label a political map of Europe with the countries and capitals.
   Read Chapter 26 on pages 280–295 of your *World Geography* book and complete the exercises at the end of the chapter.

Part 2: Pick two of the following activities from the choices below.

1. Hand draw and label a physical map of Europe using an appropriate key and colors.

2. Create a travel log with pictures as if you were on a train ride across Europe.

3. Write a paper about how physical features affect population density.

4. Create a tourist attraction pamphlet on the major physical features to visit in Europe.

5. Create a bar graph depicting the heights of the mountain ranges.

6. Make a commercial about what to see when you visit Europe.

7. Write a paper explaining how physical features play a role in people's lives.

8. Create your own activity (with teacher approval).

NOTE: This lesson was created by Zachary Matteson, Waterford, Michigan.

Subject: English Language Arts

Design: *Contract*

Lesson Component: *Learning Target & Student Handout*

Writer's Workshop Quarterly Contract

I, _____, agree to take on the following challenges to improve my skills as a writer this _____ quarter.

Group Mini-Lessons on Craft:

I will attend _____ group mini-lessons on craft (four minimum). Two of these will be the teacher's choice. The rest I will choose based on what I need as a writer.

Group Mini-Lessons on Grammar:

I will attend ____ group mini-lessons (four minimum). Two of these will be the teacher's choice. The others will be based on what I need as a writer.

Final Pieces of Writing to Complete:

I will complete _____ final pieces of writing (four minimum). One of those pieces must be a persuasive piece of writing.

Publishing Choices:

I plan to have my writing published in

❑ The classroom

❑ The school

❑ The local community

❑ The national community

❑ Other _____

Genres:

I plan to attempt the following genres (see genre ideas in your writer's notebook):

❑ Fiction: _____

❑ Nonfiction:_____

Classroom Community Commitments:

I understand that to be a part of the reading/writing learning community of this classroom, I must be involved in the following:

- ❏ Peer conferencing
- ❏ Teacher conferencing
- ❏ Writer's notebook
- ❏ Whole class mini-lessons
- ❏ Sharing sessions

Learning Target:

Concept: Communication

Understand That: Writers make series of decisions in determining how to communicate most effectively.

Know: Craft, conventions, genre

Able to Do:

- Revise and edit writing (both yours and others).
- Conference with peers.
- Make writer's decisions.
- Complete pieces for publication.

Now You Get It: Turn in final pieces (with drafts attached) to be assessed by the teacher

I, _____, have read and understand the target for this quarter, and I have agreed to the conditions that have been set. I will complete the expectations of this contract to the best of my ability. It is my responsibility to meet with the teacher if I wish to change anything or have any difficulties meeting the conditions of this contract.

Student Signature: _____ Date: _____

I, _____, agree to coach and guide the above named writer. I also promise to provide ideas, lessons, and an inspiring environment that will help this writer grow over the course of the quarter.

Teacher Signature: _____   Date: _____

Learning Contracts: Teaching Tips

Lesson Design

- Contracts should be a blend of skills and content-based activities.
- Note to beginners: When you first try contracts, it may be easier to begin with a whole-class contract rather than a contract for a small group or individual. As you evolve your skills, you can begin doing more complex contracts, like tiered contracts.
- As you design your contracts, think about which core activities all students will be expected to complete.
- Also think about what activities can be included in the contracts to support different learning profiles and interests.
- Decide how you will weight each task in the contract. Will you assess everything? Which items best reflect your objectives? Will they all have the same weight or not?

Management

- Allow students to determine the plan for completing their contracts by the assigned dates. They can determine what they want to work on as class work or as homework.
- If students do not fulfill their contract obligations, have them sign a Student Responsibility form. (See the "Resources" section.) Students can also help you determine the consequences for not completing their contracts.
- Be sure to have an anchor activity for students to work on if they get done early.
- When students complete their contracts, have them paperclip completed assignments together with the contract on top. Have a basket for each class period's work.
- Expect and encourage students to help each other before coming to you for help. (*"See three before me."*)
- Create three-sided table tents labeled, "Hard at Work," "HELP!" and "Finished." Students turn their tent to reflect where they are on their contract, so you can look around the room to see what they need. (Be sure to check the finished work to see if it is quality work before allowing students to move to anchor activities.)
- Begin the class by checking in with students to make a plan for the day's work session. Students should take some time to set a daily goal for working on their contract. It helps to have a plan in place for students who need to leave the class and for how to manage and share materials.

Assessment

- Exit cards are a great tool for having students self-assess while working on contracts. (See examples in this chapter and in the "Resources" section.)
- If you have several activities listed on a contract, tell students you will be assessing them on having all the assignments completed and that you will grade one assignment of their choice and one that you will select randomly. This helps you manage the amount of paperwork you have to correct.
- You could give a traditional quiz or test at the end of the lesson or unit.
- **Teacher Self-Assessment:** As you try out contracts, reflect on what's working and what is not working. For example, if some students are not living up to their contracts, have them sign a Student Responsibility form.

11

Deep and Dynamic Design #5

Learning Stations

Teacher Overview

Concept: Varying learning profiles

Understand That (Key Principles)

Stations provide interest and challenge for all types of learners.

Know (Facts)

- Stations are areas set up around a classroom. Students rotate to different stations to explore new topics or practice skills.
- Stations can be designed based on process or products.
- Stations can be differentiated by readiness level. For high ability learners, stations can give them opportunities to broaden their knowledge and go deeper into a topic. For struggling learners, stations can be adapted to provide remedial work.
- Stations can be developed around different learning styles and intelligences.

- Structured stations are stations where students learn objectives through specific tasks. Management rules are set and workspace is provided. Structured stations allow learners to work on specific applications of a lesson or unit and to practice a skill independently.
- Exploratory stations are stations where students explore ideas and objectives through discovery, creating, solving problems, inventing, and manipulating at their own pace and understanding.

Able to Do (Skills/Be able to . . .)

- Students may rotate to each station and try each activity, or students may be assigned to specific stations developed to meet specific needs.
- Depending on the complexity of the stations, the teacher may need to do some preteaching before the students go to the stations.
- Station tasks should be active and engaging for all types of learners.
- The teacher needs to move about from station to station to monitor the students and make adjustments if needed.
- Students may reflect on what they learned in the stations through logs, self-assessments, or short quizzes.

Now You Get It!

Learning stations will:
- Provide fun, active, and engaging ways to learn information.
- Help students be more independent in their learning.
- Offer a great way to incorporate technology.

Content Examples

Subject: Mathematics

Design: Stations

Lesson Component: Learning Target & Planning Guide

Inequalities Learning Stations

Concept: Relationships

Understand That:

Mathematicians use numerical formulas to show relationships between numbers.

Know:

- The steps for solving inequality problems
- Mathematical equations have sequences or patterns
- When you know how the sequence or pattern works, you can solve the problem

Able to Do:

- Solve inequality problems

Now You Get It:

- Final test on inequalities
- Daily center behavior: Students turn in exit cards
- Upon center completion, students share mnemonics with the class

Station 1 Title: Number Mnemonics

Objectives Met: Know the steps for solving inequalities

Materials Needed:

- Handout: Number Mnemonics
- Markers and paper

Structured or *Exploratory*

Station 2 Title: Problem-Solving Station (This station will be tiered)

Objectives Met: Able to solve inequality equations

Materials Needed:

- Levels of problems for low, middle, and high groups run off on different colored paper for each tier
- Answer keys

Structured or Exploratory

Station 3 Title: Solving Story Problems Station

Objectives Met: Mathematicians use numerical formulas to show relationships between numbers.

Materials Needed:

- Story problems at varying levels of complexity run off on different colors of paper for each tier
- Answer keys

Structured or Exploratory

Lesson Component: Student Handout

Solving Story Problems Station

1. Solve the story problems listed on the handout in this station.
2. Check your answers.
3. If you get an answer wrong, figure out where you went wrong and rework the problem until you get the correct answer.
4. If you can't get the problem correct, get someone in your group to help you figure it out.
5. Want more challenge? Try creating some of your own story problems. Check your answers on a calculator. Make an answer key for the problems you created.

Lesson Component: Student Handout

Number Mnemonics Station

1. Break down, in writing, the steps for solving algebra inequality problems.
2. Now, using a multiple intelligence strength, create a mnemonic that will help someone with your MI strength to remember the steps for solving equations.
   a. Music Smart? Create a song, rap, or poem.
   b. Art Smart? Draw a poster or graphically represent the terms.

    c. Body Smart? Be the numbers, and act out the problem, or do some other kind of skit or movement related activity.

    d. Word Smart? Create an acrostic or word trick.

    e. People Smart? Find a way to get lots of people engaged in learning the steps.

    f. Self Smart? Create your own, just for you, unique way of remembering the steps.

3. Relate your mnemonic to an actual math problem.

At the end of the hour, plan to share what you have created.

Lesson Component: Student Handout

Problem-Solving Station

1. Solve the problems listed on the handout in this station.

2. Check your answers.

3. If you get an answer wrong, figure out where you went wrong and rework the problem until you get the correct answer.

4. If you can't get the problem correct, get someone in your group to help you figure it out.

5. Want more challenge? Try creating some of your own inequality problems. Check your answers on a calculator. Make an answer key for the problems you created.

Lesson Component: Student Handout

Algebra Exit Card: Self-Assessment

Date _____

Name _____

	Low				High
1. I used my station time wisely.	1	2	3	4	5
2. I understand how to solve inequalities.	1	2	3	4	5
3. I had a positive attitude.	1	2	3	4	5

I still need help on . . .

_____

_____

_____

_____

_____

What I learned was . . .

_____

_____

_____

_____

_____

Subject: Science

Design: Stations

Lesson Component: Learning Target & Student Handout

Roots, Stems, and Leaves

Learning Stations

In the learning stations for this unit of study, you will choose the ways you will meet these objectives:

Understand That:

An organism's structure enables it to carry out life functions in its particular environment.

Know:

- Terminology: Structure, function
- Adaptations of plant roots, stems, and leaves

Able to Do:

Observe plants' structural characteristics, experiment to discover the relationship between structure and function, research adaptations, and summarize similarities and differences between plant parts.

Now You Get It:

After completing all stations, turn in your work with the "Independent Plan" stapled to the top. I will assess you on your understanding of the learning target based on the quality and accuracy of the activities you chose.

Background:

- There are six stations set up in the lab area: two for roots, two for stems, and two for leaves. Each station has a unique set of activities that will help you come to understand the importance and functions of each of these plant parts.
- For each set of stations, there is one that contains traditional activities such as labs, worksheets, and question sheets: these are "House Plants" stations. The other station explores more unconventional ways of learning, such as poetry, song, mobiles, and models: these are "Wild Weeds" stations.
- Each activity at each station has a total point value. (Remember, just because you complete an activity does not mean you will earn all the points—*Do quality work!*) You must earn 30 points at each station. Choose which activities will best get *you* to 30 points.

Directions:

1. Spend ten minutes today looking around at the various activities, and choose the ones you would like to do this week.
2. Fill out the "Independent Plan" on the back of this sheet. This will be your table of contents, so do not lose it. You will refer to it at the beginning and end of each day.
3. Beginning tomorrow, you will float between the stations at your own pace, completing the activities you chose for that day. You do not have to stay at one station the whole day.
4. Watch the clock!!! You have only four full days to complete three stations (probably doing three activities at each station).
5. Some of the work should be taken home for homework. You decide when it is necessary to take work home so that you can meet your goals.
6. Read directions carefully. Some of the activities have requirements or limits on them.
7. Everyone is required to do *one lab*, and this can be with a partner (total of two people).
8. Everyone is required to do one activity from each "type" of station. For example, if you feel very comfortable with "House Plant" type stations, you must do one activity from a "Wild Weed" station to expand yourself outside of your comfort zone. ☺

Lesson Component: *Student Handout*

Independent Plan

Station	Activity Description	Points	To Be Completed On	✔

Roots

Station: House Plants

1. Research mangrove trees. Describe their root system. Why is it unique? What type of environment do they live in? Why are the roots an adaptation to that environment? (10 points)
2. Watch the filmstrip on roots. Write five good questions and answers from the filmstrip. (5 points)
3. Complete the front and back of the skills worksheet. (10 points)
4. Complete the lab at this station. You may work with a partner. Prepare ahead of time by reading through the lab thoroughly. (15 points)
5. Complete the acrostic worksheet. (5 points)
6. Complete the "Reading Questions" based on pages 312–314. (5 points)

Roots

Station: Wild Weeds

1. Create a rap to remember any five parts of the root and their importance. (10 points)
2. Create a picture dictionary including five of the following terms: epidermis, cortex, cambium, pith, root cap, and apical meristem. The pictures must be labeled and in color. (5 points)
3. Make your own diagram of the major parts of a root and label those parts. Include what you feel are the five most important parts. (5 points)
4. Create a mobile using a coat hanger with pictures and descriptions of different root systems (taproots, fibrous roots, adventitious roots). (10 points)
5. Develop a menu where roots are the main ingredients. (5 points)
6. Write a poem entitled "Ode to a Root Hair." (5 points)
7. Write a short story *or* create a storyboard describing a trip from the epidermis to the inside of a root and the sites you would see along the way. (10 points)

Stems

Station: House Plants

1. Make a Venn diagram contrasting two types of stems: herbaceous and woody. (5 points)
2. Watch the filmstrip on stems. Write five good questions and answers from the filmstrip. (5 points)

3. Complete the front and back of the skills worksheet. (10 points)
4. Complete the lab at this station. You may work with a partner. Prepare ahead of time by reading through the lab thoroughly. (15 points)

5. Create a jumble word puzzle with clues using terminology from page 154. You should include eight jumbled words. (5 points)
6. Complete the "Woody Stem Observation" activity (10 points)
7. Complete the Challenge worksheet which requires some research in the library. (5 points)

Stems

Station: Wild Weeds

1. Develop a menu where stems are the main ingredients. (5 points)
2. Create a picture dictionary including five terms related to stems. The pictures must be labeled and in color. (5 points)
3. Make your own diagram of the major parts of a stem and label those parts. Include what you feel are the five most important parts. (5 points)
4. Create a cartoon titled "How Stem Saves the Day," describing the importance and function of the stem. (10 points)

5. Develop a public service announcement (like a commercial) promoting the importance of stems in our lives (pretend the audience is a bunch of plants). You may perform this in front of the class at the end of the week or record it at home and show it to me later. (10 points)
6. Write a love letter to a stem explaining how it is more important than the root to you and why you are leaving the root for the stem. (We all know that they are equally important ☺.) (10 points)
7. Create five newspaper headlines announcing how outstanding stems are to a plant; include the functions of stems. (5 points)

Leaves

Station: House Plants

1. Complete the coloring for leaves provided at this station. (5 points)
2. Complete the worksheet on modified leaves. (10 points)
3. Complete the front and back of the skills worksheet. (10 points)
4. Complete the lab at this station. You may work with a partner. Prepare ahead of time by reading through the lab thoroughly. (15 points)

5. Complete the acrostic worksheet. (5 points)
6. Complete the "Reading Questions" based on pages 314–316. (5 points)
7. Create three tongue twisters about the functions of parts of leaves. (5 points)

Leaves

Station: Wild Weeds

1. Create a picture dictionary including five terms related to leaves. The pictures must be labeled and in color. (5 points)
2. Make your own diagram of the major parts of a leaf and label those parts. Include what you feel are the five most important parts. (5 points)
3. Create a mobile out of a coat hanger showing pictures and descriptions of different leaf arrangements. You may want to use the Internet or an encyclopedia for additional information. (10 points)
4. Create a three-dimensional model of parts of a leaf (10 points)
5. Create five analogies for the relationship between stomata and guard cells. (5 points)

6. Draw three plants for each of the following environments: dry, hot desert; intertidal swampy area; cool northern forest. Write a brief description of adaptations that each plant has to possess to survive in its environment. (10 points)

Subject: Social Studies

Design: *Stations*

Lesson Component: *Learning Target & Student Handout*

Ancient Greece Study Stations

Concept: Culture

Understand That*:*

- Studying past cultures helps us to understand our own culture.
- The political thinking and actions of a culture affect the populous in positive or negative ways.

Know:

- The geography of ancient Greece
- The culture of ancient Greece

Able to Do:
- Read, research, and gather data
- Write a myth

Now You Get It:

- Complete projects should be placed in folders at each station.
- At the end of the station time, I will collect from you and assess . . .
  - One piece of your choice from the completed centers
  - One piece of my choice from the completed centers

Station 1: Greek Myths

(**Able to Do:** Students will create their own myth)

Choose one person to read *The Story of Arachne* and one person to read *King Midas.* Discuss the two Greek myths. Write your own myth. Make sure you put your name at the top of your paper. Add your paper to the back of this center's folder before moving on to the next center.

You may use one of the following topics to get started, or think of a topic of your own:

- Why do we have clouds in the sky?
- Why is the grass green?
- Why are there ants?
- Why does the sun rise and set?

Station 2: Greek Geography

(**Know:** Students will know how the geography of ancient Greece impacted the culture and economy)

Work independently to complete the "Ancient Greece" worksheet. If you do not complete it during your time at this center, take it home to complete it.

Station 3: Greek Government

(**Understand That:** Students will understand how the political thinking of the time affected the populous)

From our readings and class discussions, discuss, with your group, the tyranny, aristocracy, and democracy that existed in ancient Greece and how each affected the populous. Use the graphic organizer to organize your findings. Write a short piece or draw a picture (*Do quality work!*) connecting what you learned about the government in Greece to what you know about the government today. How are the current government's decisions affecting the people of today?

Remember to write your name at the top and to add your writing or picture to the back of the folder before you move to the next center.

Station 4: Cultural Comparisons

(**Understand That:** Studying past cultures helps us to understand our own culture.)

We have studied a lot about ancient Greek culture. Take an area of this culture that you were most interested in and compare and contrast it to the same part of our culture. You can explain your comparison by (1) making a Venn diagram or another compare/contrast chart; (2) writing a poem, song, or rap; or (3) making a cartoon or children's book.

File your completed comparison in the folder of this center. If you don't finish during class time, you can take this home to complete it.

NOTE: These stations were created by Tara McMillan, Illinois.

Subject: English Language Arts

Design: *Tiered stations—Students grouped into three groups by readiness levels*

Lesson Component: *Learning Target*

Learning Target

Concept: Communication
As a result students should . . .

Understand That:

- Writers use a variety of sentence structures in order to keep the reader engaged and interested.
- Writing skills improve through the practice of writing techniques.

Know:

- Simple and complete subjects and predicates
- Compound subjects
- Sentence combining

Able to Do:

- Identify and create sentences of various lengths and structures.
- Combine sentences.
  Station 1: Sentence combining
  Station 2: Copy change
  Station 3: Students edit own writing and combine sentences, or students create a piece of writing that shows a variety of long and short sentences

---

Lesson Component: *Student Handout*

Combining Station

1. On a separate sheet of paper, try combining into one sentence at least five of the sentences in your folder.

2. Go over your sentences with someone else to see if you have combined the sentences in different ways. Check for correct punctuation of your sentences.

3. If you finish early, challenge yourself with more complex sentence combining exercises.

You Write Station

1. Imagine a situation, real or imagined, that you are experiencing with someone else. (For example, imagine going fishing with your dad, going to a party with friends, sharing a special time with a grandparent, or making a discovery with a sibling.)

2. Now, write a short piece about that experience. Be aware of using longer and shorter sentences. Try to create a mood with the long and short sentences.

3. After you have completed your draft, go back to see if there are any places where your writing would be stronger if you combined sentences.

4. Share your piece with someone else.

Copy Change Station

Copy change at least three fairly long sentences from published authors. EXAMPLES:

Original Sentence:
There was a crowd of kids watching the car, and the square was hot, and the trees were green, and the flags hung on their staffs, and it was good to get out of the sun and under the shade of the arcade that runs all the way around the square.—Ernest Hemingway
Copy Change:
There was the audience watching my every move, and the stage lights were hot, and my stomach felt queasy, and the collar of my costume was too tight around my neck, and it felt wonderful to get away from center stage and into the cool darkness that resides beyond the spotlight and behind the black curtains.

Original Sentence:
Nearly ten years had passed since the Dursleys had woken up to find their nephew on the front steps, but Privet Drive had hardly changed at all—J. K Rowling
Copy Change:
Almost three years had gone by since Joy had lived to find her house destroyed by the giant wind, and the neighborhood had changed in so many ways.

Now meet with someone else and discuss how the authors *could* have written these long sentences as many short choppy sentences, and why you think the authors made the choices that they did. Complete the exit card for this center, and turn it into your teacher.
CHALLENGE: See if you can make all your copy-changed sentences connect into one idea. You can add some shorter sentences in between for sentence variety.

Lesson Component: *Student Handout*

Copy Change Station Exit Card

NAME_____

	Low				High
1. I used my time wisely in this station	1	2	3	4	5
2. I understood what to do in this station.	1	2	3	4	5
3. I had a quality discussion with others about using sentence variety	1	2	3	4	5

Tell why you think writers need to know how to write a variety of sentence structures:

_____

_____

_____

_____

_____

Learning Stations: Teaching Tips

Lesson Design

- Note to beginners: When you first try stations, it's easier to begin with fewer, less-complex centers. As you develop your skills, you can begin doing more complex stations, tiered stations, and so on.
- You may create different stations that each meet a different C U KAN objective.
- You could combine structured stations with exploratory stations.
- Stations can be tiered. Students can be grouped by readiness levels and then rotate through the centers. If you color code the groups by readiness level (red, blue, green), you can match the handouts at the center to the color and readiness level of each group.
- It's impossible to make sure that all stations take the same amount of time. Be sure to have anchor activities for students to work on if they finish early.

Management

- Use an overhead timer or Time Timer™ so that students can keep track of how much time they have at the station. Use chimes, a gong, a whistle, or other signal to let the groups know that it's time to change stations.
- Again, be sure to have an anchor activity for students to work on if they get done early.
- Appoint a station leader who makes sure that the center is reorganized before his or her group moves on to the next center.
- Expect and encourage students to help each other before coming to you for help. (*"See three before me."*)

Assessment

- Students should be clear about the *Understand*, *Know*, and *Able to do* components that they are learning at each station.
- When students work in stations, exit cards are a great tool for student self-assessment. (See examples in this chapter.)
- You can determine what you want to collect and grade from the stations. You may choose to collect only one finished piece from a station (but not inform students about which one you plan to assess) or you could have mini-tasks that you collect from each station.

- You could give a traditional quiz or test about what they learned in the stations.
- **Teacher Self-Assessment**: As you try out stations, reflect on what's working and what is not working. For example, if some students are not able to handle being in stations, have a plan for pulling them out and giving them an alternative assignment to work on that day.

12

Deep and Dynamic Design #6

Compacting

Teacher Overview

Concept: Challenge

Understand That (Key Principles)

- Advanced learners need to experience academic challenge.
- Advanced learners need to learn to take risks and persevere on tasks.

Know (Facts):

- Compacting is a strategy that differentiates for high ability students.
- Compacting involves three basic steps:

    1. The teacher assesses what students already know about the material to be studied.

    2. A plan is made for students to skip what they already know and to learn what is not known.

3. A plan is made for students to use the available time to accelerate their study or enrich their learning.

Able to Do (Skills/Be able to . . .)

- Students are given a pretest to determine what they already know about the unit to be studied.
- Students who score 85%–90% or above on the pretest are expected to complete an alternative study or project.
- Students who test out are accountable for learning materials they did not know on the pretest.
- Students are expected to sign a contract with expectations for task accomplishment during class time. Students complete a daily work log.
- Students may share their projects or research with the rest of the class.
- Students who compact may choose to work on group projects.

Now You Get It!

Compacted lessons will:
- Allow high ability students to move more quickly through the curriculum
- Provide challenges and eliminate boredom
- Enable teachers to accelerate advanced students using a simple and organized format

Content Examples

Subject: Mathematics

Design: Compacting

Lesson Component: Learning Target & Student Handout

Geometry Study Guide

Choose an alternative topic from the list provided, and follow the conditions of the independent study contract.

Understand That:

- Mathematicians look for patterns and classify information in order to communicate and make sense of the world.

Know:

- Formulas for finding perimeter, area, and volume of various polygons
- Applications for perimeter, area, and volume of various polygons

Able to Do:

- Estimate volumes, perimeters, and areas
- Compute volumes, perimeters, and areas

You will be expected to take the class quizzes for the above objectives. The dates for the quizzes will be as follows:

Quiz #1 _____

Quiz #2 _____

Quiz #3 _____

Lesson Component: Rubric

Compacted Geometry Rubric

Expectations	Amazing!	Above Average	Average	Additional Effort Needed
Understand ✓ Mathematicians look for patterns and classify information in order to communicate and make sense of the world. _____ Points	❏ Shows complex understanding and extension of the concept _____ Points	❏ Understands the concepts and explores ideas beyond facts and details _____ Points	❏ Limited understanding of key concepts and little depth or elaboration _____ Points	❏ Little understanding of the concept _____ Points
Know ✓ Formulas for finding perimeter, area, and volume of various polygons ✓ Applications for perimeter, area, and volume of various polygons _____ Points	❏ Uses correct formulas to solve problems ❏ Applies accurate knowledge to new situations and problems with ease _____ Points	❏ Uses correct formulas to solve problems ❏ Applies accurate knowledge to new situations with minimal support _____ Points	❏ Uses correct formulas most of the time ❏ Limited ability to use formulas to extend to new situations _____ Points	❏ Has difficulty using correct formulas ❏ Little ability to use formulas in new situations _____ Points

(Continued)

(Continued)

Expectations	Amazing!	Above Average	Average	Additional Effort Needed
Quality and Creativity (list three choice activities) 1. _____ 2. _____ 3. _____ _____ Points	☐ Met quality work criteria ☐ Unique, fresh, or imaginative work _____ Points	☐ Met quality work criteria ☐ Creatively integrates work _____ Points	☐ Met quality work criteria _____ Points	☐ Does not meet quality work criteria _____ Points

What I/we did that was quality work: _____

What I/we would do better next time: _____

Student Grade: _____   Teacher Grade: _____

Comments:

154

Subject: Science

Design: *Compacting*

Lesson Component: *Student Handout*

Compacted Unit: Scientific Investigation and Experimentation

Background: Many of you are very familiar with the scientific method and the proper way to conduct experiments and ask questions. Since you passed the pretest with an 85% or better, you have the option of extending your knowledge of scientific investigations and deepening your understandings. You are accountable for quizzes along the way to monitor your growth and also for any additional assignment that will help you with the material that you did not pass on the preassessment. Keep these targets in mind:

Concept: Questioning

Understand That: Scientists make scientific progress by asking meaningful questions and conducting detailed investigations.

Know: Hypothesis, theory, tools used in investigations (probes, graphing calculators, lab equipment), how to identify controls, variables

Able to Do: Analyze relationships from data, formulate explanations, identify inconsistent results, research literature

Procedure:

- Decide which questions you had difficulty with on the pretest, and confer with me about a course of action to solidify that learning.
- Choose ONE of the following projects to present to the class on the day before the traditional assessment. The presentation and additional materials you turn in will serve as your assessment. Be sure to use the rubric to guide your planning and follow-through.
- Each day (five days), fill out the study log to assess how you are keeping on track and how you can improve. Provide detailed comments on what you accomplished, and then rate yourself, using a scale of 1–5 (5 being the highest), on how you are keeping on track. Reflect on your progress, and come up with at least two ways you can push yourself more sometime during the week.
- Enjoy! Challenge yourself!

Choice of activities:

- Study cancer research. How important are controls and variables to the research? How important is having a detailed plan? What role do numerous retests play in cancer research? Discuss the consequences of errors in research. Briefly describe some of the lab equipment used in tests. Describe how new discoveries in the past ten years have changed the course of cancer research.
- If you choose this activity, you will receive some sample data gathered from a stream in Tennessee on salamander lengths, tail lengths, and sample location. Using this data, what conclusions can you draw (there are many)? How can you present the data in two forms other than the table given? Develop a hypothetical test you could conduct on the salamanders, and describe it in detail, including control samples.
- Research one scientific finding in our past that has changed scientific thinking. Discuss the pathway that lead to the new finding. Why was the old belief held for so long? Also, give an example of a change in a theory that occurred through many small discoveries. How did each of the "baby steps" contribute to the significant change in thinking?
- Your choice. Is there something that you are passionate about, that you've always wondered, that you want to understand more about? Let's take a look at it and see where you can go!

Independent Work Log

Date	Daily Work Plan	Work Actually Completed				
		Comments:				
		1	2	3	4	5
		Comments:				
		1	2	3	4	5
		Comments:				
		1	2	3	4	5
		Comments:				
		1	2	3	4	5
		Comments:				
		1	2	3	4	5
		Comments:				
		1	2	3	4	5

Lesson Component: Rubric

Expectations	In a league with Isaac Newton	Could be an assistant to Isaac Newton	Might go to Isaac Newton for tutoring	You and Isaac could share a sundae sometime
Understand ✓ Scientists make scientific progress by asking meaningful questions and conducting detailed investigations 15 Points	☐ Shows complex understanding of the concepts ☐ Explores related ideas ___ Points	☐ Understands the concepts ☐ Explores ideas beyond facts and details ___ Points	☐ Limited understanding of key concepts ☐ Little depth or elaboration of idea ___ Points	☐ Little understanding of the concept ___ Points
Know ✓ Terms: Hypothesis theory, controls, variables ✓ Tools used in investigations (probes, graphing calculators, lab equipment) 15 Points	☐ Precise facts ☐ In depth and well supported ☐ Knows all terms and tools; able to discuss how they are used ___ Points	☐ Covers facts effectively ☐ Well developed ☐ Knows all terms and tools used in investigations ___ Points	☐ Valid facts but little depth or elaboration ☐ Knows most terms ☐ Identifies some tools; little elaboration on how they are used ___ Points	☐ Needs more facts ☐ Needs accurate facts ☐ Needs assistance with terms; no knowledge of investigative procedures ___ Points
Quality Work 10 Points	☐ Unique, fresh, or imaginative work ___ Points	☐ Creatively integrates work ___ Points	☐ Met objectives with minimal quality ___ Points	☐ Did not do quality work ___ Points
Habits of Mind Working independently, monitoring and adjusting, challenging yourself 10 Points	☐ Highly resourceful ☐ Quality effort ☐ Completed contract beyond expectations ___ Points	☐ Resourceful ☐ Good effort ☐ Completed contract successfully ___ Points	☐ Minimally resourceful ☐ Minimal effort ☐ Met minimal expectations of contract ___ Points	☐ Not resourceful ☐ Little or no effort ☐ Contract incomplete ___ Points
What I/we did that was quality work				
What I/we would do better next time				

Subject: Social Studies

Design: *Compacting*

Lesson Component: *Student Handout*

Latitude and Longitude Unit: Alternative Projects

You have demonstrated in your quick write that you already know the essential learning related to longitude and latitude, so you may choose two of the following mini-projects to work on for the next two weeks to gain credit for this unit. You will be graded on quality, accuracy, and creativity. You will still be expected to take part in "Economic Fridays."

Concept: Challenge

Understand That: Lifelong learners grow from taking on appropriately challenging learning experiences.

Know:

- Perseverance
- Risk taking

Able to Do:
- Self-select a project
- Work on it to completion

1. Geography Picture Book

Using the major terms associated with latitude and longitude, create a picture book showing the meaning and a picture of at least 20 major terms. (Computer PowerPoint Presentation could also be done.)

2. Papier-mâché

Using papier-mâché, create a globe of the world and label all the major lines of latitude and longitude. Take the globe, and cut it so it will lay flat and show what effect distortion has upon a round object. Make a poster showing some examples of different projection maps and what types of distortions they have. List the advantages and disadvantages of each type of map.

3. Book Report

Read two books with settings in different climate zones. On a world map, locate the setting of the book by using latitude and longitude. In a report, describe what effect the zone of latitude has upon the plots of the books. Using two Venn diagrams, show how physical and cultural geography are different or the same in the two books.

4. Bulletin Board

Using the bulletin board in the hallway, create a learning center on latitude and longitude. Show the tools a geographer uses, posters showing the major lines, and examples of how to predict and estimate lines of latitude. What effect does the tilt of the earth have upon the climate?

5. Role Play

Investigate the life of an early geographer. What major contributions did she or he have upon the study of geography? Where did the geographer live? What time period? How did this person come up with a new geographical idea? Did others readily accept this idea? Present to the class your findings as this famous geographer visiting from back in time.

Lesson Component: *Student Handout*

Student Contract for Advanced Learning Opportunities

Student Name: _____

Having tested out of a unit, I promise to do the following:

- I will select and complete an alternative assignment that is challenging for me.
- I will use my time wisely each day and record my daily efforts in my "Log of Project Work."
- If I need help, I will wait until the teacher is not busy.
- If no one can help, I will try to keep working or move to another activity.
- I won't bother other students or the teacher. I will not brag about my work.
- I will complete the projects I choose to do and turn them in to the teacher.

Student Signature: _____ Date _____

I agree to help this student follow this plan.

Teacher Signature: _____ Date _____

Lesson Component: *Student Handout*

Date	*Daily Work Plan*	*Work Actually Completed*

SOURCE: This lesson was designed by Robert Benhke, Huron Valley Schools, Milford, Michigan.

Subject: English Language Arts

Design*: Compacting*

Lesson Component*: Learning Target & Student Handout*

Language Arts: Advanced Learning Contract

Nonfiction

_____ For an A grade on my nonfiction project, I will do the following:

❑ Gather information from both primary (firsthand) and secondary (secondhand) sources. I will have a minimum of four different sources.

❑ I will present the information I have gathered in a unique and creative way.

❑ I will use top quality visuals and/or audiovisuals.

❑ I will take the knowledge I have gained and evaluate or synthesize that knowledge in a new way.

_____ For a B grade on my independent project, I will do the following:

❑ I will use mostly secondary sources, and I will have a minimum of three sources.

❑ I will present the information I gathered.

❑ I will have visuals and/or audiovisuals.

❑ I will be sharing the new knowledge I have gained at the application or analysis level.

Fiction

_____ For an A grade on my fiction project, I will do the following:

❑ Select a fiction genre I have wanted to try writing.

❑ Find at least three models of that type of writing, and study the author's craft.

❑ Try using two of the craft techniques I learned from other authors.

❑ Sketch out a map or brainstorm of my own piece. Keep all my drafts and notes.

❑ Take the piece through to a final draft and submit it to a writing contest or publisher

_____ For a B grade on my independent project, I will do the following:

❑ Select a fiction genre I have written before.

❑ Find one model of that type of writing and study the author's craft.

❑ Try using one of the craft techniques I learned from another author.

❑ Have some evidence of how I grew my piece (e.g., first draft, some notes).

❑ Take the piece through to a final draft.

The project I plan to work on is . . .

Student Signature: _____

Teacher Signature: _____

Student Contract for Advanced Learning Opportunities

Student Name: _____

I have chosen to test out of some of my class work and complete other tasks at my own pace. As a result, I have bought myself time to work on an independent learning project.

Student: I agree to the following:

1. I will select and complete an alternative assignment that is challenging for me.

2. I will use my time wisely each day and record my daily efforts in my "Log of Project Work."

3. If will set up conference times with my teacher to review my work.

4. I will be respectful of others and not brag about my work.

5. I will complete the projects I choose to do and turn them in to the teacher.

Student Signature: _____ Date: _____

Teacher: I agree to help this student follow this plan.

Teacher Signature: _____ Date: _____

Concept: Challenge

Understand That: Lifelong learners grow from taking on appropriately challenging learning experiences.

Know:

- Perseverance
- Risk taking

Able to Do:

- Take a risk by selecting a project that will challenge you.
- Develop perseverance by working on a project to completion.

Compacting: Teaching Tips

Lesson Design

- Compacting is for students who can pass a pretest to show that they already know the C U KAN for the lesson. Activities should then be designed to deepen the students' knowledge within the C U KAN objectives.
- Note to beginners: When you first try compacting, you may want to offer fewer options regarding what students can do with the time they have bought. As you evolve your skills, you can begin offering more choices or letting the students design the choices.
- As you plan the compacted activities, think about ways to support different learning profiles and interests.
- Some compacted lesson designs include choice menus, orbital studies (independent, long-term studies), and student-designed projects.

Management

- Students who compact out of the unit must sign a contract regarding their obligations for working independently. If students do not fulfill their contract obligations, they are brought back with the rest of the class.
- Students might also contract for the grade they are going to work for on their projects.
- Students need to keep a daily log of work accomplished and report to you daily by using an exit card or attending a brief conference.
- If students are going to be working away from your classroom, be sure that another adult is aware of where the students are supposed to be.

Assessment

- Exit cards are great self-assessment tools for students working on compacted assignments. (See examples in this chapter.)
- The pretest grade can be averaged with the grade students earn on their projects.
- You can require students to take any quizzes or final tests that the rest of the class is taking. Students will be expected to prepare for the test on their own time.
- **Teacher Self-Assessment:** As you try out compacting, reflect on what's working and what is not working. For example, if you have too many students testing out of a unit, you may need to rethink your preassessment. Generally, only around the top 3% of your class should be able to pass a pretest.

PART III

Evaluating and Committing to the Inspiring Classroom

13

Assessment and Grading in the Inspiring Classroom

"Those who have most at stake in the old culture, or are most rigid in their beliefs, try to summon people back to the old ideas."
—Marilyn Ferguson

Let's listen to Ms. Johnson, a teacher in an inspiring classroom, to see how she uses assessment as an ongoing tool for evaluating her students before, during, and after learning.

"Okay class, we'll be starting the new unit on the environment. Before we get started, I'd like to see what you already know, so I'm going to have you do a quick write on a half sheet of paper. For the last seven minutes of class, I would like you to write whatever you think you know about the pollution problems in our environment, types of pollution, and what people are or should be doing to help the environment. You can add diagrams and drawings if you like. You will turn in this exit card to me as you leave class today."

(A few days later) "I have gone over your quick write exit cards, and I noticed that you all have a pretty good background and understanding about issues concerning the environment. So, I figured this would be a great time to offer you some choices about what you study and how you present what you learn. Here are the target objectives for the unit. (The C U KAN objectives are written on chart paper at the front of the room.) Let's go over them together because you will need to include the *Understand* and *Know* learning targets in whatever project you decide to do." (During the discussion, students brainstorm and Ms. Johnson notes questions and misconceptions the students have about the learning targets.)

"Your *Able to do* skill for this unit is note taking. Note taking is one of the vital know-hows that lifelong learners need, so I will be modeling and showing you how to take notes as you research in preparation for your final project. Be sure to remember that, on the final rubric for this project, you will get points for turning in your notes and for the quality of those notes." (Ms. Johnson models the process and scaffolds the instruction of note taking as students gather data from various sources. She "kid watches" over the next few days, observing how students are progressing at taking notes and gathering data for their projects.)

"Now, class, you have spent the last few days taking notes and becoming experts on the area of pollution you have chosen to study. Remember that your project needs to meet the objectives for this unit. I would like you to look over your notes and, for five minutes, discuss with your learning partner how well you understand and know the learning targets for this unit. After five minutes, I'll ask for a 'thumbs up' on how you are doing." (After five minutes, students give a thumbs up if they've got it, a sideways thumb if they have some but not all of the information, and a thumbs down if they are not getting it. From this information, Ms. Johnson determines who needs more help, who might be willing to help others, and who's doing fine.)

(On the final day of the project, Ms. Johnson again discusses assessment.) "It's time for the *Now you get it!* part of the project. Today you will be presenting or turning in your final project for the environmental unit. Take out the rubric you received a few days ago. Recall that you are being graded on how well you present the *Understand* and *Know* objectives in your project, the quality of your project, and your notes. Now it's time for you to reflect on how well you think you have met these objectives. As you self-assess using the rubric, you should be thinking, 'How do I think I did? How do I think that compares to Ms. Johnson's opinion?' You also need to reflect on what you feel you did that was quality work and what you would do better next time. I will then assess and grade your project using the same rubric. Since I am the final evaluator for this project, it will be my grade that goes in the grade book. I am excited to see your final results."

As you can see, Ms. Johnson created her lesson with the end in mind, so she was able to plan engaging and meaningful ways to help her students succeed in meeting those objectives. She preassessed her students to see where their skills and knowledge were strong and where they were lacking. During learning, she used the preassessment information to help her effectively *Chunk*, *Chew*, and *Check* her lesson. She continued to assess and provide feedback to both the whole class and individual students during the learning process. The students were expected to reflect upon and internalize what they needed to do to grow their skills. The students did a final self-reflection using the rubric that the teacher also used as a final assessment. This ongoing assessment is an essential component of the inspiring classroom.

It is important to note that assessment and grading *are not the same*. Assessment occurs throughout learning. It is an ongoing process for collecting data about students in order to make sound instructional decisions. Assessment occurs in many forms and includes students' self-reflecting about their own learning. Grading occurs at the end of learning. It is how we communicate our final judgment about how successful each student has been at hitting the learning target. Grading and assessment are made easy when we use the C U KAN framework to define our learning target clearly. The C U KAN framework also makes it easy for us to provide ongoing feedback to students and for students to self-assess during learning.

Ongoing Assessment

Assessment in the inspiring classroom is the continuous process of gathering data about our students before, during, and after learning. This ongoing assessment keeps us, and our students, informed of progress, which allows for more efficient and effective use of our instructional time. When we are informed, we no longer have to make a best guess about our students' needs or hope that the class understands our lesson. We *know* what our students need, and we *know* whether they are on target or not. Listed below are ideas for assessing before, during, and after learning.

Assessment Before Learning

Once we have established the learning objectives (C U KAN) for our unit, we can honor our students by determining their interests, attitudes, and learning styles as well as by preassessing to find out what they already know. (See Figure 13.1.)

Reasons for assessing before learning:

- To determine students' differences *before* planning lessons
- To make decisions about the best options for differentiating for our students

- To get information about the interests, learning styles, and readiness levels of students
- To identify starting points for instruction
- To identify who already knows and who has gaps
- To allow for more efficient use of instructional time (see Figure 13.1)

Assessment During Learning

Once we have established our learning objectives and preassessed our students, it is time to monitor their growth toward the targeted objectives. This is also the time to teach students to self-reflect on their own growth toward meeting the objectives. (See Figure 13.2.)

Reasons for Assessing During Learning:

- To monitor and adjust students' work
- To give students feedback from us, their peers, and themselves
- To help students before the grading of a lesson or unit, when it may be too late
- To help students reflect realistically on where they are in their understanding of the learning target

Assessment After Learning

Once the learning process is complete, we do a final assessment, or grade students, to measure how well they hit the learning target. (See Figure 13.3.)

Reasons for Assessing After Learning:

- To find out what students have learned about a topic
- To teach students to reflect on their growth as learners
- To evaluate where students are in their thinking and learning
- To fulfill the obligations of grading according to the curriculum and of communicating those grades to students and parents or guardians

Grading in the Inspiring Classroom: Now They Get It!

Grading is always a hot topic as we learn to reach and teach all types of learners. To gain clarity about the purpose for grading, there are questions we may want to ponder regarding what and how we measure students' learning.

Figure 13.1   How to Assess Before Learning

To determine	Use	Examples and Information
How best to deliver and assess the content you are about to teach	Student learning styles profile	See "Resources" section for examples.
What interests and/or attitudes students have about the content you are about to teach	Content-related interest survey	See "Resources" section for examples.
What students know and understand about the content you are about to teach	Quick write	Have students discuss, write, map, draw what they think they already know before you begin.
	Teacher-prepared pretests for global concepts	Students who know 80% or above on a pretest should be given alternative work, such as an independent contract. Students with little or no background knowledge need to build more prior knowledge as they study the unit.
What misconceptions students might have about the content you are about to teach	Teacher observation checklists	Make a checklist of observable skills needed and check off your observations. Use the data to form focus learning groups.
	Students' product and work samples	Review a current piece of work, using your C U KAN framework, to look for indicators of what students already know, understand, or are able to do for an upcoming unit.
	Squaring off	Students can either move to signs posted in the room, or you can have them jot down their level and you can collect these. **Pro** – I know enough about this topic that I could teach it to others. **Top Player** – I know a lot; enough to know there's more. **Rookie** – I have some knowledge, but need to learn a lot more. **Amateur**– I don't know much about this topic.
What critical thinking skills students currently possess	Anticipation guides	Students respond to a set of agree/disagree statements related to a lesson. Their predictions give indications of their background knowledge on the subject.
	Traffic light	Give students the objectives of the unit and either green, red, or yellow stickers or markers. If they think they know the objective well, they mark it green. If they have some knowledge, but not a lot, they mark the objective yellow. If they don't know much, they mark it red.

Figure 13.2   How to Assess During Learning

To Determine	Use	Examples and Information
If you need to adjust students' work	Kid watching	Teacher observes behaviors of students working on projects, makes notes, and provides feedback when appropriate. Post-it notes are great for giving immediate feedback. Students love to read the messages we write to them.
If students need help before the grading of a lesson or unit (when it may be too late)	High five	On a scale of 1–5, how well do I know this? (Students can jot the number down or hold up the number of fingers that shows where they are in their understanding.) • I could teach it to others. • I can do it on my own. • I need some help. • I could use more practice. • I am just learning this.
If students are reflecting on what they know, understand, and are able to do	Thumbs up!	Students raise thumbs up if they know a lot about what they are learning. Students turn thumbs sideways if they know some, but not all, about what they are learning. Students turn thumbs down if know very little about what they are learning or if they are lost.
	Exit cards	Students fill out exit questionnaire cards, reflecting on where they are in understanding and knowing the learning objectives of the unit. Teachers read and assess. (See the "Resources" section for exit card examples.)
	Traffic light	Same as in preassessment, but students add green, red, or yellow dots to show how they have grown in their learning since the pre-assessment.
	Quiz	We can give students a mini-quiz at various points in the unit. Students should assess themselves or each other and use the information from the quiz to reflect on what they know and still need to learn.

If we grade to measure whether or not our students "got it," are we doing so in ways that are fair to all learners? Is it fair for us to expect our students to show understanding in the exact same way now that we clearly recognize that our students learn differently? Should our students be graded on individual growth or against a standard measure of achievement? Is it fair to compare a student with learning challenges to a student who is a gifted learner? When teachers use traditional grading practices, it is possible for gifted students to get "A's" without really trying hard or learning anything. At the same time, we have students with learning challenges who work

Figure 13.3 How to Assess After Learning

To Determine if Students	Use	Examples and Information
Have mastered facts Have memorized information or Can recall details	True/False Multiple-choice tests Fill in the blank	1. What year did the ___ begin? a. b. c. 2. A decimal and a _____ represent the same proportion.
Have acquired thinking skills Can apply reasoning or Have developed a deep understanding	Open or constructed response Essay questions	1. What were major factors that influenced the beginning of the American Civil War? _____ 2. Compare and contrast *Romeo and Juliet* with *West Side Story*.
Have mastered a skill or ability Can structure and apply skills Have acquired thinking skills Can apply reasoning or Have developed a deep understanding	Performance-based demonstration of ability	**Choice Menu** Make a poster, present a lesson, or perform a skit. **Real Application** Send a persuasive letter to your member of Congress. Develop a marketing campaign to sell tickets for the junior talent show.
Recognize their own understanding of the learning Recognize their strengths	Student self-assessment, reflection, and goal setting	**Portfolios:** Students collect work, usually in a folder, and periodically reflect on their progress over time, identifying evidence of growth and making a plan for future learning. **Student-Led Conferences:** Students plan a conference time to meet with parents and the teacher to discuss how they have learned. **Rubrics and Reflections on Quality of Work** What I did that was quality What I would do better next time

their tails off only to receive a "D," when, in truth, they have progressed more than the advanced student. So does a single score really reflect our students' learning?

In the world outside school, we need to gain knowledge, experience accomplishments, and develop a work ethic to succeed. So perhaps a more fair and equitable way to measure what students have learned would be to measure for three criteria: (1) How well a student has mastered the content, (2) How much progress a student has made, and (3) What quality of work habits the student is developing.

Some visionary school districts are actually making the move toward powerful grading reform as suggested by Carol Ann Tomlinson and Jay

McTighe (2006) in their new book, *Integrating Differentiated Instruction + Understanding by Design*. For example, Crystal Lake District 47, a suburb of Chicago, Illinois, has based its electronic grading system on the following three sets of criteria: (1) Progress—How much students have gained from their learning experience, (2) Product—What students know and are able to do as related to the learning standards, and (3) Process—What tools students are developing to make their learning gains. (See the Web site www.d47schools .org). This grading system allows the district's teachers to clearly communicate whether students have made any growth from where they started; are functioning above, at, or below grade level; and are developing learning skills and effective habits of mind. A grading system like this offers students and parents far more useful feedback than a single grading system does.

If our districts have not yet made the major shift toward a more equitable, informative grading system, we can still begin to shift our own paradigm about grading. Here are some thoughts and suggestions as we move toward inspiring assessment and grading:

- If we begin our units and lessons by developing our C U KAN framework, and clearly defining what we want students to *Understand*, *Know*, and be *Able to do*, then we can more effectively design the *Now you get it!* component of our lessons to match those criteria. For example, we are able to design our choice menus much more effectively when we create them with the learning target in mind. Choice menus don't work very well when we design random, "fun" choices without first considering what we expect students to show in their final product.
- Traditionally, teachers tend to weight tests heavily in the final grade. While this is great for students who test well, it isn't so great for students who are not good test takers. If we balance differentiated grades with traditional tests, we allow the top kid to be at the top, but the struggling learner or weak test taker does not always have to be at the bottom. Until districts stop comparing students, a balanced grading approach allows us to report student success and individual growth. Figure 13.4 illustrates this balanced grading system.

Figure 13.4   Sample Student Grades

	Test	*Project*	*Test*	*Homework*	*Project*	*Test*	*Final*
Alex	98	89	95	97	93	100	95%
Susie	76	88	75	88	92	70	82%

Note that Susie doesn't test as well as Alex. She is able to show her understanding better when she does projects. By balancing Susie's test grades with her project grades, the teacher enables Susie to reach a higher level of success in the class. This balanced grading system honors Susie's strengths. A balance between traditional assessments and differentiated assessments creates a more fair and realistic report of what our students have learned.

Assessing Our Own Growth

When we work to create an inspiring classroom, it's important that we also reflect upon and assess our own growth. As teachers, we have a tendency to be hard on ourselves. We often expect that our lessons should turn out right the first time. We also have limited time and energy for creating the perfect lesson to teach every day. How do we move ourselves forward without beating ourselves up?

Here are some suggestions for getting started, for growing our skills, and for being patient with ourselves in the process.

Start Small. You Don't Have to Do It All. Start at Your Comfort Level.

- Gather one piece of data about your students and organize it into a user-friendly format. (See Chapter 3)
- Implement some ideas from Chapter 3 to create the environment and set the tone in your classroom.
- Try some lite-n-lean strategies from Chapter 5. They are easy to do, and, when you see how much the students enjoy learning this way, you'll be motivated to try some of the more advanced designs.
- Design one deep and dynamic lesson per quarter from Chapter 6. These lessons do take time to design well, but if you set a goal to design one per quarter, you will start to build a repertoire of quality lessons. Design four more lessons the following year, and see your repertoire of engaging and meaningful lessons grow!

Collaborate With Others

- It's much more fun to write lessons and discuss ideas with other teachers.
- Set a goal to get together with colleagues once a quarter to write a C U KAN lesson or unit. Note how powerful your thinking and your lessons become when you put your heads together!

Make Time for Reflection

- No matter how wise you are, or how long you've been teaching, you will go through five stages in learning to change and grow your practice. There *will* be risk taking and mistake making involved. In learning to teach this way, all of us will grow though these stages.
  - Unconsciously incompetent
  - Consciously incompetent
  - Consciously competent
  - Unconsciously competent
  - Reflective competence

- These lessons rarely come out right the first time you teach them. (Believe us, we speak from experience on this point!) When you try a lesson and it does not go well, rather than saying to yourself, "This doesn't work in my classroom" you can ask, "Hmmm, I really liked the way many of my students responded to this lesson, but what can I do to fix that management problem (or better assess the outcomes or whatever)." "Let me see . . . I think they would work better in their groups if I gave them jobs like 'Leader' and 'Recorder.' Then I think I need to have them make up a list of tasks needed to complete the project and have them commit to which part they are going to complete."
- The C U KAN lesson planner in the "Resources" section has a built-in reflection section where you can jot down what you want to change for the next time. Building this simple reflective habit will have a great affect on growing your skills.

It's Okay Not to Know, But Once You Know, It's NOT Okay Not to Grow

- If we expect our students to be risk takers, then we need to model risk taking ourselves. Now that we know some new techniques, we need to take a risk and try them out! We can have some fun with this. Remember, if *we* are having fun teaching, it is very likely that our students are having fun learning!

As we look at our students and envision the type of human beings we want them to be in this world, it is clear that they learn more from us than, "What do you know?" We are also helping them to be able to reflect on progress toward goals and to develop lifelong learning habits that empower them beyond school. In the inspiring classroom, we know we must have a way to report this information to our students, to show them we see their growth beyond the content standards. We recognize and honor the skills they are developing. If we don't, we are likely to lose them. Assessment and grading must recognize that students learn at different rates and show growth in many ways. This more encompassing and informative system honors all the ways that humans grow.

Opening the Door

Creating an Inspiring Legacy

"Hold on to people, they're slipping away."
—Moby

Now is the time for us to take bold steps as middle school and secondary educators. We are losing too many of our students to apathy, boredom, and failure. By high school, as many as 40% to 60% of all students—urban, suburban, and rural—are chronically disengaged from school (Klem & Connell, 2004). Now more than ever, our students need us to honor them as individuals. They deserve to learn in a safe and inviting community. They have a right to be taught information that is relevant to their world. So let us open our classroom doors, enter our classrooms, and be inspired by the faces of the learners who surround us. Be joyfully curious about our students as people as well as students. Be open to all the possibilities they bring to our learning community. Be willing to take risks and make mistakes to make learning come alive in our classroom.

We create the legacy we leave for our students. Will we create a legacy of inspiration or a legacy of complacency? The choice is ours. We can choose to experience the joy of knowing our students, the richness of learning in a community, and the power of connecting students' lives to the depth of our content, or we can choose to cover content and teach as if one size fits all. If we choose to pass along a legacy of inspiration, we lead our students to discover their own greatness. Because they have seen themselves as contributors in our inspiring classrooms, they will see themselves as contributors in creating a better world. And the world will be a better place. What greater legacy could we possibly leave?

You ARE a Marvel

Each second we live in a new and unique moment of the universe, a moment that will never be again. . . .

And what do we teach our children?

We teach them that two times two makes four, and that Paris is the capital of France.

When will we also teach them what they are?

We should say to each of them: Do you know what you are?

You are a marvel.

You are unique.

In all the years that have passed, there never was another child like you.

Your legs, your arms, your clever fingers, the way you move.

You may become a Shakespeare, a Michelangelo, a Beethoven.

You have the capacity for anything.

Yes, you are a marvel.

And when you grow up, can you then harm another who is like you, a marvel?

You must work, we must all work, to make the world worthy of its children.

—Pablo Casals

Resources

How to Use the Resources:

The resources are designated by an alphabetical and numerical component. The alphabetical component represents a group of similar resources. For example, B.3 and B.5 are student surveys. The numerical component signifies the sequence within the group of similar items and helps navigate the reader through that section.

A. Overview
  1. The Big Picture
  2. Goal Setting

B. Student Surveys and Questionnaires
  1. Multiple Intelligences Survey
  2. Sternberg Processing Preference
  3. Learning Styles Inventory
  4. General Interest Inventory
  5. Specific Content Knowledge and Interest Inventory
  6. Learning Preferences Questionnaire

C. Resources for Working With Groups
  1. Group Contract
  2. Group Processing Sheet
  3. Group Behavior Chart

D. Bibliography for Vital Know-Hows

E. At-a-Glance
  1. Anchor Activities
  2. Ways to Chunk, Chew, and Check

F. C U KAN
  1. Examples of Understandings
  2. Learning Target Template
  3. Planning Guide Template

G. Example Lesson (Environment) Written in Each Dynamic Design
  1. C U KAN for ALL Lesson Designs
  2. Choice Design
  3. RAFT Plus
  4. Tiered Lesson
  5. Contracts
  6. Learning Stations
  7. Compacting

H. Lesson Templates
 1. Tic-Tac-Toe
 2. Cubing
 3. Destination Dice
 4. RAFT Plus

I. Lesson Planning Guides & Example Handouts
 1. Designing a Student Contract
 2. Student Work Contract
 3. Work Log
 4. Planning Learning Stations
 5. Curriculum Compacting Guidelines

J. Assessment
 1. Quality Work Rubric
 2. Exit Cards
 3. Criteria for Quality Work
 4. Rubric (detailed)
 5. Rubric (simplified)

K. Further Reading
 1. General
 2. Varied Level Texts

A.1 The Big Picture

Creating an Inspiring Classroom:
Meeting the Needs of All Learners

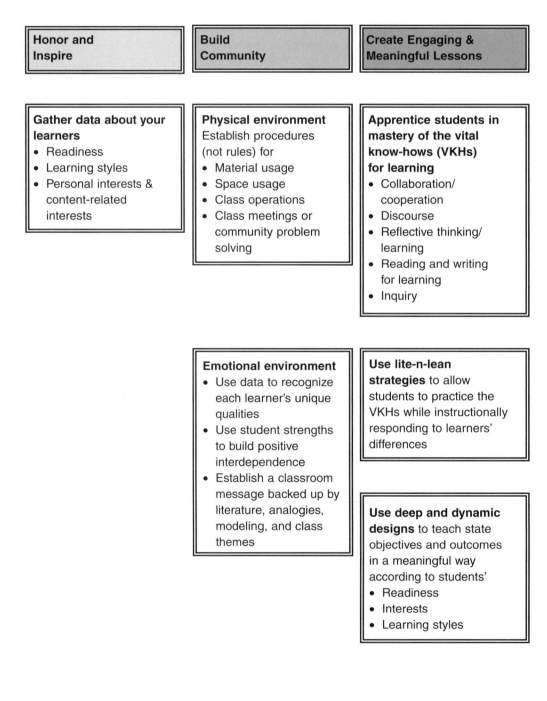

Honor and Inspire

Build Community

Create Engaging & Meaningful Lessons

Gather data about your learners
- Readiness
- Learning styles
- Personal interests & content-related interests

Physical environment
Establish procedures (not rules) for
- Material usage
- Space usage
- Class operations
- Class meetings or community problem solving

Apprentice students in mastery of the vital know-hows (VKHs) for learning
- Collaboration/ cooperation
- Discourse
- Reflective thinking/ learning
- Reading and writing for learning
- Inquiry

Emotional environment
- Use data to recognize each learner's unique qualities
- Use student strengths to build positive interdependence
- Establish a classroom message backed up by literature, analogies, modeling, and class themes

Use lite-n-lean strategies to allow students to practice the VKHs while instructionally responding to learners' differences

Use deep and dynamic designs to teach state objectives and outcomes in a meaningful way according to students'
- Readiness
- Interests
- Learning styles

A. 2 The Big Picture: Goal Setting

Honor and Inspire	Build Community	Create Engaging & Meaningful Lessons

| Gather data about your learners

Goal: | Physical environment

Goal: | Apprentice students in mastery of the vital know-hows (VKHs) for learning

Goal: |

| | Emotional environment

Goal: | Use lite-n-lean strategies

Goal: |

| | | Use deep and dynamic designs

Goal: |

B.1 Multiple Intelligences Survey

How Are You Smart?

DIRECTIONS: Below you will find listed the eight types of intelligence. Listed under each intelligence are some descriptions of activities that relate to that type of intelligence. Read the descriptions, and check the boxes that describe you. Go with your first instinct. Then total the number you checked at the bottom of each intelligence section. At the end, transfer each total to the Multiple Intelligence Rubric to see what your strongest intelligences are. Remember, most people are strong in more than one intelligence. Have fun! ☺

Intelligence #1

___ I can hear or see words in my head before I speak, read, or write them.

___ I like games such as Scrabble, Jeopardy, Trivial Pursuit, word searches, and crossword puzzles.

___ I enjoy writing and have received praise or recognition for my writing talents.

___ I often talk about things that I have read or heard.

___ I love to read books, magazines, anything!

___ I am good with words. I learn and use new words in creative or funny ways regularly.

___ When I am in a classroom, I pay attention to all the written posters and the writing on the board.

___ I have a very good memory for hearing and seeing words.

Intelligence #2

___I enjoy activities like dancing, swimming, biking, or skating.

___I play a sport or do physical activity regularly.

___I need to do things with my hands or by moving in order to learn best.

___I am good at imitating others and like drama and acting.

___ I use my hands and body when I am talking with someone.

___ I need to move around a lot and change positions often when sitting.

___ I need to touch things to learn about them.

Intelligence #3

___I like to draw and doodle.

___I am good at finding my way around places I don't know well.

___I can easily see in my head how furniture would fit in a room. I am also good at jigsaw puzzles.

___ I remember things better if I can draw or create an image of them.

___When I look at paintings or pictures, I notice the colors and shapes and how objects are spaced.

___I prefer learning from pictures.

___I picture things in my mind.

Intelligence #4

___I listen to music or have music playing in my head most of the time.

___I play a musical instrument or have a good singing voice.

___ I can easily pick up rhythms and can move to them or tap them out.

___ I can easily remember or create songs.

___ I often make tapping sounds or sing while working or studying.

___ I can remember things better if I put them in a song.

___ I can hear all the parts when I listen to music.

Intelligence #5

___ Math is one of my favorite subjects.

___ I like to play games such as chess, Clue, or Stratego.

___ I like to do scientific experiments.

___ I like to calculate, measure, and figure things out.

___ I enjoy brainteasers and puzzles.

___ Using a computer comes easily to me. I understand how they work and can spend time learning about them.

___ I see patterns in things.

Intelligence #6

___ I understand and can express feelings about myself.

___ I enjoy spending time by myself.

___ I like to work alone.

___ I am comfortable having ideas and opinions that are not the same as those of others.

___ I feel good about who I am most of the time.

___ I have a realistic view of my strengths and weaknesses.

___ I enjoy playing games and doing activities that I can do by myself.

Intelligence #7

___ I have many friends.

___ I enjoy playing group games and team sports.

___ I enjoy working in groups and tend to be the leader in the group.

___ I really care about others and try to understand how others feel and think.

___ I feel comfortable being in the middle of groups or crowds.

___ I enjoy teaching another person or a group of people something that I know how to do well.

___ I like to get involved in social activities in school, church, or the community.

Intelligence #8

___ I like to watch and observe what is going on around me.

___ I think about the environment a lot and want to make sure that we don't pollute our planet.

___ I like to collect rocks, leaves, or other nature items.

___ I feel best when I am out in nature.

___ I understand how different plants and animals are connected to each other.

___ I can easily get used to being in new places.

___ I like to organize things and put them in categories.

(Continued)

Multiple Intelligence
Scoring Rubric

Circle the number that you scored in each section of the survey. You are smartest in areas where you scored 5–7 points.

      Weak   Strong

Intelligence #1: Word Smart (Linguistic)

| 1 | 2 | 3 | 4 | 5 | 6 | 7 |

Intelligence #2: Body Smart (Bodily-Kinesthetic)

| 1 | 2 | 3 | 4 | 5 | 6 | 7 |

Intelligence #3: Art Smart (Spatial)

| 1 | 2 | 3 | 4 | 5 | 6 | 7 |

Intelligence #4: Music Smart (Musical)

| 1 | 2 | 3 | 4 | 5 | 6 | 7 |

Intelligence #5: Math Smart (Logical)

| 1 | 2 | 3 | 4 | 5 | 6 | 7 |

Intelligence #6: Self Smart (Intrapersonal)

| 1 | 2 | 3 | 4 | 5 | 6 | 7 |

Intelligence #7: People Smart (Interpersonal)

| 1 | 2 | 3 | 4 | 5 | 6 | 7 |

Intelligence #8: Nature Smart (Naturalistic)

| 1 | 2 | 3 | 4 | 5 | 6 | 7 |

My strongest areas of intelligence are:

_____

_____

I need to build my strengths in these areas:

_____

_____

B.2 Sternberg Processing Preferences

All of us process, or make sense of information, in different ways. I am curious to know, and more important, I want *you* to understand how you think about things. When given a new problem, something to solve, or to connect to, how do you make sense of that new information? Below you will find some scenarios. Read the responses to each scenario, and check the one that most accurately describes how you would approach it.

Situation 1

You are trying to convince your parents to let you go on a teen retreat in two weekends. In the discussion you most likely would

- ☐ A. Present them with a schedule of activities
- ☐ B. Make the connection between this weekend and future responsibilities that you will soon face
- ☐ C. Create a dialogue between two fictional characters in which your ideal solution plays itself out

Situation 2

You are going to try out for the school play or sports team. Do you . . .

- ☐ A. Practice, practice, practice
- ☐ B. Analyze the odds of making the cut, and study people who have succeeded
- ☐ C. Visualize yourself making it

Situation 3

In marketing class, you are chosen as team leader for a project to advertise a new product for the local ice cream shop. You most likely would

- ☐ A. Pull out a legal pad and start making a list of what needs to be done to accomplish the task
- ☐ B. Contact another local ice cream shop to see what they have done in the past for advertising a new product
- ☐ C. Take on the role of a small child who often comes to this shop to see the shop from the child's viewpoint—What would make children want to ask their parents to go to this shop?

(Continued)

Situation 4

You are asked to make a decision for your team about the uniform they should order for next season. You most likely would

☐ A. Make a list of pros and cons for three different uniforms
☐ B. Research current trends in sports uniforms and their function to see which is best
☐ C. Create a design of your own

Situation 5

You are at a friend's house, listening to some tunes on her iPod. You hear a new song by a new artist. You most likely would

☐ A. Ask who the artist is, where he originated, how long he has been in music, what his musical background is. You want all the details!
☐ B. Find out if local clubs are playing this music. Look into what audience is listening to this music.
☐ C. Think how you could use the song for a skit you are preparing for science class or how the lyrics connect to an upcoming paper you are writing for English class. You want to incorporate into your life!

Situation 6

You have a major project coming up in your most challenging class. Do you

☐ A. Break the project into smaller tasks and create a calendar for completion of each task
☐ B. Research how others have been successful in getting a good grade on the project and utilize their processes
☐ C. Decide to create your project like no one else has ever done before

SCORING: Tally the number of A's, B's, and C's and read the interpretation at the end.

_____ A's

_____ B's

_____ C's

Interpretation:

If you checked mostly **A**'s, you are an ANALYTICAL thinker. You probably like details and thinking sequentially; on tests or assignments, you may process best through activities that involve judging, comparing and contrasting, and evaluating.

If you checked mostly **B**'s, you are a PRACTICAL thinker. You probably like to focus on the use and application of new learning; on tests or assignments, you may process best through activities that involve trying it out, putting it into practice, and demonstrating.

If you checked mostly **C**'s, you are a CREATIVE thinker. You probably like to think outside of the box and ask "what if" questions; on tests or assignments, you may process best through activities that involve inventing, imagining, creating, and predicting.

If you found you had an equal distribution of answers, you most likely have several ways to process information. Start noticing when you use creative thinking, practical thinking, or analytical thinking to find out which style works best for you in different learning situations.

B.3 Learning Styles Inventory

Everyone learns differently. Learning styles are the ways that we are able to take in and make sense of new information. Of the six different learning styles, most people have one or two that are their strengths. However, you may have a combination of several styles that you use for learning. Answer each question below with the response that *best* describes how you take in and think about new information. At the end, tally your score and read the interpretation.

_____1. To make sense of new learning, it helps me to
    a. talk about it
    b. think about it
    c. read about it
    d. write about it
    e. hear about it
    f. work with it

_____2. I do best in classes where teachers
    a. let me work in small groups and discuss new ideas
    b. let me have some quiet time to process and visualize new learning
    c. let me read about new information before lectures
    d. let me journal about my thoughts and questions
    e. lecture on new information
    f. design an activity for me to do: draw, construct, experiment

_____3. If I need to get directions to a new place, I prefer to
    a. repeat the directions verbally
    b. see the map in my mind
    c. read the written directions
    d. write the directions down for myself
    e. listen to someone give me directions
    f. grab a map and figure it out

_____4. If the teacher draws a diagram on the board, I make sense of it by
    a. talking about it with a friend
    b. seeing the picture
    c. reading some text that discusses the concept
    d. writing down the major ideas
    e. remembering what the teacher said about it
    f. drawing it for myself

_____5. If I need to learn how to spell a new word, I will
   a. say it over and over again to myself
   b. visualize the letters in my mind
   c. look at it on paper
   d. write it a few times
   e. spell it out loud to hear if it sounds right
   f. use my fingers to trace the letters in the air

Interpretation of the Learning Styles Survey

I had the most number of _____

If you had three or more A's, one of your strongest learning styles is **speaking**. You learn best by expressing yourself out loud.

If you had three or more B's, one of your strongest learning styles is **visualizing**. You learn best when you have a picture in your mind.

If you had three or more C's, one of your strongest learning styles is **reading**. It is easy for you to read about things and remember and understand them.

If you had three or more D's, one of your strongest learning styles is **writing**. You express yourself easily through writing.

If you had three or more E's, one of your strongest learning styles is **listening**. It is easy for you to acquire new information by hearing it.

If you had three or more F's, one of your strongest learning styles is **manipulating**. You learn best by manipulating objects and moving things around.

If no letter occurred more than the others, you have a balanced learning style and can acquire and process information in many ways.

Honor the way you learn. When you are given a choice of how to take in new information, use this knowledge of the strengths you have and use your learning style to own the new learning!

B.4 General Interest Inventory

NAME: _____   DATE: _____

1. What is your favorite subject to learn about in school? (Check all that apply)

   ❑ Writing   ❑ Geography
   ❑ Reading   ❑ History
   ❑ Physical Education   ❑ Science
   ❑ Art   ❑ Math
   ❑ Literature   ❑ Computers
   ❑ Other: _____

2. What do you enjoy the most about school? What do you enjoy the least about school?

   _____

   _____

3. Do you prefer to work   A. Alone   B. In groups   C. Both (Circle One)

4. What hobbies and special interests do you have (e.g., sports, clubs, collections, activities)? Be specific.

   _____

   _____

5. What do you like to do when you have free time?

   _____

   _____

6. How much time do you spend watching TV each week?
   _____ What do you watch?

   _____

7. How much time do you spend on the computer each week?
   _____ What do you like to do on the computer?

   _____

8. What types of music do you listen to? _____

9. What should a teacher know about you that will help you learn best in school?

   _____

10. What is the most important thing to you in your life? What are your future goals?_____

    _____

12. What is something that you do really well and that you are most proud of?

    _____

    _____

B.5 Examples of Specific Content Inventories

Science—Newton's Laws of Motion

Rank these categories (1 = top choice) to show what you are most interested in studying during our unit on Newton's Laws of Motion.

____ Car racing

____ Theme parks

____ Machines

____ Architecture

____ Musical instruments

____ Sports (pole vault, football)

History—Civil War

Which topics of the Civil War are you most knowledgeable about?

____ Causes

____ Effects

____ Battles

____ Heroes

____ Strategies

When comparing causes of the Civil War to political issues today, would you prefer to

____ debate   ____ present

____ perform   ____ write

____ display

Math Geometry Unit

Which do you like better

____ Practical geometry

____ Theoretical geometry

Rate the following in order of personal enjoyment using 1 (high) through 3 (low)

____ Solving geometric equations

____ Drawing geometric figures

____ Discovering the history of geometry

Literature—Shakespeare's Life and Times

What would you like to learn about Shakespeare's writings as a reflection of his life and time period?

____ Culture

____ Religion

____ His life story

____ Social norms

____ Geography

____ Government/Politics

B.6 Learning Preferences Questionnaire

How Do You Like to Learn?

1. I study best when it is quiet.	Yes	No
2. I am able to ignore the noise of other people talking while I am working.	Yes	No
3. I like to work at a table or desk.	Yes	No
4. I like to work on the floor.	Yes	No
5. I work hard for myself.	Yes	No
6. I work hard for my parents or teacher.	Yes	No
7. I will work on an assignment until it is completed, no matter what.	Yes	No
8. Sometimes I get frustrated with my work and do not finish it.	Yes	No
9. When my teacher gives an assignment, I like to have exact steps on how to complete it.	Yes	No
10. When my teacher gives an assignment, I like to create my own steps on how to complete it.	Yes	No
11. I like to work by myself.	Yes	No
12. I like to work in pairs or in groups.	Yes	No
13. I like to have an unlimited amount of time to work on an assignment.	Yes	No
14. I like to have a certain amount of time to work on an assignment.	Yes	No
15. I like to learn by moving and doing.	Yes	No

C.1 Group Contract

This contract is hereby entered into by:

_____   _____

_____   _____

on this day, _____

We hereby call ourselves _____

Certain responsibilities and expectations come along with the opportunity to work closely with our peers. Some of these responsibilities and expectations include

1._____

2._____

3._____

4._____

In addition to the above mentioned, we each will be a critical part of the team and have committed to fulfilling one of the following roles:

- **Team Coach** _____

This person has the important role of keeping the team on track. You should keep the group on task, make sure every person understands what the assignment is, and ask questions when the assignment is not clear. Of primary importance: at the beginning of each class period, see that all people in your group are filling out their agendas based on the class agenda at the front of the room.

- **Materials Manager**_____

This responsible and organized person should complete three main goals: (1) Before class begins, gather for the team materials that the teacher has set up for the day's lesson; (2) pass out corrected work or papers from the class period folder; and (3) turn in papers for the group, including homework, tests, or work the teacher would like to see for the day.

(Continued)

- **Record Keeper**_____

This person should be an excellent summarizer who is capable of recording details. You will (1) maintain notes in the group work log, (2) record the groups' task list for the next day's work, and (3) organize the group processing sheets or group behavior chart, whichever your group chooses to use.

- **Group Reporter** _____

A person of strong moral character and excellent communication skills should be assigned to this position. You are responsible for maintaining the makeup folder for your group, which will include (1) daily notes from the Record Keeper of the team, (2) extra worksheets or copies for missing team members, (3) group processing sheets or behavior chart. Also, you will meet with me to discuss how your group is doing and share your group processing sheets or behavior chart.

I, _____, have entered this agreement with trust. I have placed much responsibility upon each of you to help make this class a first-rate class. If there are any issues within your group that you cannot *first* resolve among yourselves, then please see me, and we will work them out together. I trust that you will contribute your part. If you feel that you cannot carry out your responsibility, speak up in your group before signing your name.

About once a week, we will rate ourselves as to how the team is functioning. If all is going well, the group may choose to keep the same person doing the same job. If, however, someone is not upholding *this* contract that *all* agreed to, then group members may switch positions. Good luck!

Signed _____

Date _____

C.2 Group Processing

Group Processing Sheet

I completed my group job today.	Yes	No
I contributed ideas to the group.	Yes	No
I helped others if they needed my assistance.	Yes	No
I worked my best to solve problems with others.	Yes	No

Group Processing Sheet

I completed my group job today.	Yes	No
I contributed ideas to the group.	Yes	No
I helped others if they needed my assistance.	Yes	No
I worked my best to solve problems with others.	Yes	No

Group Processing Sheet

I completed my group job today.	Yes	No
I contributed ideas to the group.	Yes	No
I helped others if they needed my assistance.	Yes	No
I worked my best to solve problems with others.	Yes	No

Group Processing Sheet

I completed my group job today.	Yes	No
I contributed ideas to the group.	Yes	No
I helped others if they needed my assistance.	Yes	No
I worked my best to solve problems with others.	Yes	No

C.3 Group Behavior Chart

Name of Group:

After determining your group expectations for this task, rate your group from 1–5 each day for each group behavior. (One is the lowest; five is the highest.)

Group Expectations	Date	Date	Date	Date	Date

D. Vital Know-Hows Bibliography

Biancarosa, C., & Snow, C. E. (2006). *Reading next—A vision for action and research in middle and high school literacy: A report to* the *Carnegie Corporation of New York* (2nd ed.). Washington, DC: Alliance for Excellent Education. Retrieved May 7, 2006, from http://www.all4ed.org/publications/ReadingNext/index.html.

Billmeyer, R., & Barton, M. I. (1998). *Teaching reading in the content areas: If not me, then who?* Aurora, CO: McREL.

Daniels, H., & Zemelman, S. (2004). *Subjects matter: Every teacher's guide to content area reading.* Portsmouth, NH: Heinemann.

Harvey, S., & Goudis, A. (2000). *Strategies that work.* York, ME: Stenhouse.

Horowitz, R. (Ed.). (1994). *Classroom talk about text: What teenagers and teachers come to know about the world through talk about text.* San Antonio, TX: International Reading Association.

Jensen, E. (1998). *Teaching with the brain in mind.* Alexandria, VA: Association for Supervision and Curriculum Development.

National Research Council. (1999). *How people learn: Brain, mind, experience and school.* Washington, DC: National Academy Press.

Rothstein, E., & Lauber, G. (2000). *Writing as learning.* Thousand Oaks, CA: Corwin Press.

Schoenbach, R., Greenleaf, C., Cziko, C., & Hurwitz, L. (1999). *Reading for understanding: A guide to improving reading in middle and high school classrooms.* San Francisco: Jossey-Bass.

Sejnost, R., & Thiese, S. (2001). *Reading and writing across content areas.* Thousand Oaks, CA: Corwin Press.

E.1 Middle School/High School Anchor Activities

Language Arts	Math
• Silent reading • Journaling • "Guinness Book" scavenger hunt • "Brain Quest" • Create own "Brain Quest" questions • Word analogy games and puzzles • Word wall bulletin board • Free computer time • Fluency tests • Write jingles—to help recall content • Create magnetic poetry • Mad-gabs or Mad-libs • Word sorts (parts of speech) • Sentence sequencing	• Create test questions or story problems • Do "Problems of the Week" • Create a folder of review activities • Create a folder of problem-solving activities • Puzzles and math games • Create math games • Manipulatives • Magazines (Have kids connect articles to math.) • Extended activities/Module project • Math journal writing • Research a math topic • Computer programs • Practice budgeting (holiday shopping, check book, weekly allowance)
Social Studies	**Science**
• Create vocabulary flash cards • Map activities • Board games • Create brochures or guides • Summarize chapters in *fun* ways (TV guide) • Independent reading (historical fiction) • Create a mini-activity menu • Create a crossword puzzle • Journal • Write a song to help you learn • "Brain Teasers" • Design a monument • Create a play or skit • Write a biography about your historic hero	• Mini-lab centers • Science "Question of the Week" • Learning log • Read science articles • Create a mini-experiment • Science puzzles and games • Draw vocabulary pictures • Create a review game • Act out vocabulary • Add to "Science in the News" board • Write content songs • Add illustrated words to the word wall • Add to class timeline • Write scientist biographies

Miscellaneous	Individual Inquiry
• Games and puzzles • Reading • Logic activities • Analogy activities • Mapping • Graphing • Computer time	• Computer search • Novel or short story writing • Research project • Life plan project • Social action project • Career planning • Hobby or passion
Music/Art	**Physical Education**
• Play piano with headphones • Create new rhythm pattern • Read "Music Alive" or art articles • Create rap or song or visual mnemonic for another content area • Create a new melody (choose instrument) • Research favorite music or art, musician or artist	• Practice sports drills • Walk or jog • Do stretches • Yoga or aerobics • Research a PE or health topic • Meditate

E.2 Ways to Chunk, Chew, and Check Learning

CHUNK, CHEW, and CHECK
(That's how the brain learns best!)

Chunk (Input): Vary the ways students acquire new information.

- Read the book or other, outside text
- Do a role play
- Play a game
- Watch a video
- See a presentation or demonstration
- Do an experiment
- Use technology or other media
- Class discussion
- Use tiered content—Content offered at varying readiness levels

Chew (Process): Vary learning activities or strategies to provide appropriate methods for students to explore the new concepts. It is important to give students alternative paths to process the ideas embedded within the concept.

- Do the questions
- Students design questions and share with each other
- Walk and talk about questions or prompts presented by the teacher
- Talk partners—students turn and talk to deepen understanding
- Total physical response—students learn or create movements to help them recall
- Tiered activities where students work at different levels of support, challenge, or complexity
- Centers that allow students to explore the key understandings in a variety of ways
- Developing contracts (task lists written by the teacher and containing both in-common work for the whole class and work that addresses individual needs of learners) to be completed either during specified agenda time or as students complete other work early
- Offering manipulatives or other hands-on supports for students who need them
- Using graphic organizers, maps, diagrams, or charts to display comprehension of concepts covered (vary the complexity of the graphic)
- Offering students a choice in how they want to process understanding of new vocabulary (draw, map, act out, etc.)

Check (Output): Vary how students show understanding and transfer of the learning.

- Take a quiz or test
- Tiered products or tiered quizzes or tests
- Product choice (i.e., song/rap/poem, skit/video, presentation, etc.)
- Using rubrics that match and extend students' varied skill levels
- Allowing students to work alone or in small groups on their products
- Formative ongoing assessments with students involved in self-assessing

F.1 Examples and Nonexamples of "Understandings"

As you design your C U KAN lessons, it helps to use this chart to compare examples of understandings with the nonexamples of understandings.

Examples	Nonexamples
Students will understand that examining the similarities and differences between cultures strengthens the fabric of a multicultural society.	Students will understand the culture of Latin America.
Students will understand that writers let us into their characters' minds so we can learn how internal conflicts can be handled in positive or negative ways.	Students will understand the plot, characters, and internal conflict in *The Gift of the Magi*.
Students will understand that scientists look for order and patterns to help them understand the nature of all things.	Students will understand the periodic table.
Students will understand that mathematicians look for the most efficient ways to solve problems.	Students will understand how to solve algebraic equations.
Students will understand that artists see an inanimate object from their perspective and create the image that *they* envision.	Students will understand how to paint a still life.
Students will understand that we can make sense of new content by understanding the meaning of key vocabulary.	Students will understand the key vocabulary words.

F.2 C U KAN Learning Target Template

C U KAN LESSON DESIGN LEARNING TARGET
Concept (Overarching Theme): *As a result students should . . .*   **Understand That (Key principles)**   **Know (Facts)**   **Able to Do (Skills/Be able to . . .)**   **Now You Get It!**

F.3 C U KAN Planning Guide Template

PLANNING GUIDE
Preassess: How will you determine students' readiness, interests, or learning profiles before starting your lesson or unit?
Prime: How will you engage the learners at the beginning of the lesson or unit?
Where will you be differentiating instruction? Explain how you are differentiating as you describe that section of your lesson. ❑ Chunk/Information Acquired ❑ Chew/Information Processed ❑ Check/Information Out ❑ Content/The Information **Will you be using a dynamic design for differentiating instruction? If so, which design:** ❑ RAFT Plus ❑ Choice Designs ❑ Tiered ❑ Contract ❑ Compacting ❑ Centers
Chunk: How will students acquire the new learning?
Chew: How will students get to process the new learning?
Ongoing Assessment: How will you and/or students assess during the learning?
Now You Get It! /Check for Understanding: How will students show transfer of learning?
The Information: (materials, books, Web sites, etc.)

G.1 Environment Lesson—C U KAN
for ALL Lesson Designs

LEARNING TARGET

Concept (Overarching Theme): Interactions
As a result students should . . .

Understand That (Key principles)

- All living systems are dependent upon their environment to sustain life.
- Humans must all work to keep their environment clean so that they can sustain life on the planet.

Know (Facts)

- Vocabulary: Reuse, reduce, recycle, sustainable
- Types of pollution (air, water, earth, noise)
- Ways that humans can help preserve the environment (reuse, recycle, renew, etc.)

Able to Do (Skills/Be able to . . .)

- Gather data by reading from the text, various articles, Internet sources, etc.
- Watch a video on pollution
- Work in discussion groups

Now You Get It

- Students will complete a project from a menu of projects to demonstrate their understanding.

G.2 Environment Lesson—Choice Design

Lesson Component: *Student Handout*

Name _____Date_____

Environment Choice Menu

Understand That:

- All living things are dependent upon the environment to sustain life.

- Humans must all work to keep the environment clean so that they can sustain life on the planet.

Know:

- Reuse, reduce, recycle, sustainable

- Types of pollution

- Ways that humans can preserve the environment

Now You Get It!

Using the notes you have gathered from various sources, choose one of the following ways to share what you *know* and *understand* about the type of pollution your group studied.

Environment Choice Menu

Choose one of the options below to demonstrate the *Understand, Know,* and *Able to do* components from the key learning targets about the environment.

Write a song, rap, or poem about pollution	Create a game for others to play to learn about pollution and the environment.	Create a skit or video that is a public service announcement about pollution
Your Choice:		
Create a children's book to teach children about pollution and caring for our environment	Come up with your own unique way to show what you know. (You must get the okay from your teacher first!)	Use charts and graphs to teach about the data related to pollution. Share your data and conclusions in a written or oral presentation
Design a lab that demonstrates how pollution affects the environment.	Create a news report about pollution	Using a medium of your choice, self-reflect on your own connection to the earth and the environment. Document what you observe, feel, and learn about the environment around you.

Lesson Component: Rubric

Environment Rubric

Expectations	Amazing!	Above Average	Average	Additional Effort Needed
Understand ✓ Living things depend upon the environment ✓ Humans must all work to sustain the planet 15 Points	❏ Shows complex understanding of the concepts ❏ Supports with data from text ❏ Explores related ideas _____ Points	❏ Understands the concepts ❏ Uses some text references ❏ Explores ideas beyond facts and details _____ Points	❏ Limited understanding of key concepts ❏ Limited text reference ❏ Little depth or elaboration of idea _____ Points	❏ Little understanding of the concept ❏ No or inaccurate reference to text _____ Points
Know ✓ Terms: Reuse, reduce, recycle, sustainable ✓ Types of pollution ✓ Ways to preserve the environment 15 Points	❏ Precise facts ❏ In depth and well supported _____ Points	❏ Covers facts effectively ❏ Well developed _____ Points	❏ Valid facts but little depth or elaboration _____ Points	❏ Needs more facts ❏ Needs accurate facts _____ Points
Quality Work *(as defined below by your group)* 10 Points	❏ Met quality work criteria ❏ Unique, fresh, or imaginative work _____ Points	❏ Met quality work criteria ❏ Creatively integrates work _____ Points	❏ Met quality work criteria _____ Points	❏ Does not meet quality work criteria _____ Points
Group Work/ Notes 10 Points	❏ Encourages others ❏ Collaborates and resolves conflicts _____ Points	❏ Listens well ❏ Helps others ❏ Shares _____ Points	❏ Appropriate effort ❏ Cooperative _____ Points	❏ Inappropriate effort ❏ Not cooperative _____ Points

Type of project: _____skit_____
Ways I/we will do quality work for the project:
1. Write a good script _____
2. Have costumes and props _____
3. Practice at least four times _____
Teacher Initials: _KK_ _____

What I/we did that was quality work

What I/we would do better next time

Student Grade: _____   Teacher Grade: _____

Comments:

G.3 Environment Lesson—RAFT Plus

Lesson Component: Student Handout

RAFT Plus Assignment
Garbage: A New Perspective

Role

A piece of garbage

Audience

Humans

Format

Skit, children's book, comic strip, chart or graph,

advertisement, song, your choice (see teacher for okay)

Tasks

Check these off as you add them to your project to be sure you have included everything.

_____ What types of pollution would you cause if you were not recycled?

_____ How could you be reused, reduced, and recycled?

_____ Why is it important to you and to humans that you *not* become a pollutant?

✓ You will be doing this project on your own or with one partner.
✓ You must read and gather your facts before you work on your project.

Lesson Component: *Student Handout*

Garbage: A New Perspective

Data Gathering Sheet

Name _____	
Type of Garbage _____	

What types of pollution could you cause if you are not recycled?	
How could you be reused, reduced, and recycled?	
Why should you be recycled?	
Other interesting data you want to include in your RAFT Plus	

Lesson Component: Rubric

Expectations	Amazing!	Above Average	Average	Additional Effort Needed
Understand ✓ Living things depend upon the environment. ✓ Humans must all work to sustain the planet. 15 Points	❑ Shows complex understanding of the concepts ❑ Supports with data from text ❑ Explores related ideas _____ Points	❑ Understands the concepts ❑ Uses some text references ❑ Explores ideas beyond facts and details _____ Points	❑ Limited understanding of key concepts ❑ Limited text reference ❑ Little depth or elaboration of idea _____ Points	❑ Little understanding of the concept ❑ No or inaccurate reference to text _____ Points
Know ✓ Terms: Reuse, reduce, recycle, sustainable ✓ Types of pollution ✓ Ways to preserve the environment 15 Points	❑ Precise facts ❑ In depth and well supported _____ Points	❑ Covers facts effectively ❑ Well developed _____ Points	❑ Valid facts but little depth or elaboration _____ Points	❑ Needs more facts ❑ Needs accurate facts _____ Points
Quality Work *(as defined below by your group)* 10 Points	❑ Met quality work criteria ❑ Unique, fresh, or imaginative work _____ Points	❑ Met quality work criteria ❑ Creatively integrates work _____ Points	❑ Met quality work criteria _____ Points	❑ Does not meet quality work criteria _____ Points
Group Work/ Notes 10 Points				

Type of project: _____poster_____
Ways I/we will do quality work for the project:
1. Use vibrant colors
2. Original art design
3. Unique and clear message
Teacher Initials: _KK_

What I/we did that was quality work

What I/we would do better next time

Student Grade: _____   Teacher Grade: _____

Comments:

G.4 Environmental Lesson—Tiered Lesson

Lesson Component: Student Handouts *(each card is a separate handout)*

Ecosystems: Task Card 1

Understand That (Key principles)

- All living systems are dependent upon their environment to sustain life.
- Humans must all work to keep their environment clean so that they can sustain life on the planet.

Know (Facts)

- Vocabulary: Reuse, reduce, recycle, sustainable
- Types of pollution (air, water, earth, noise)
- Ways that humans can help preserve the environment (reuse, recycle, renew, etc.)

Able to Do (Skills)

- Gather data by reading from the text, various articles, Internet sources, and so on.
- Watch a video on pollution
- Work in discussion groups
- Generate a solution to a pollution problem

Problem: Research ways your school may be creating pollution. Determine what living things in the environment might be affected by your school's pollution. Generate a solution to the pollution issue that students can participate in.

Ecosystems: Task Card 2

Understand That (Key principles)

- All living systems are dependent upon their environment to sustain life.
- Humans must all work to keep their environment clean so that they can sustain life on the planet.

Know (Facts)

- Vocabulary: Reuse, reduce, recycle, sustainable
- Types of pollution   (air, water, earth, noise)
- Ways that humans can help preserve the environment (reuse, recycle, renew, etc.)

Able to Do (Skills)

- Gather data by reading from the text, various articles, Internet sources, and so on.
- Watch a video on pollution
- Work in discussion groups
- Generate a solution to a pollution problem

Problem: Research ways your community may be creating pollution. Determine what living things in the environment might be affected by your community's pollution. Generate a solution to the pollution issue that citizens can participate in.

Ecosystems: Task Card 3

Understand That (Key principles)

- All living systems are dependent upon their environment to sustain life.
- Humans must all work to keep their environment clean so that they can sustain life on the planet.

Know (Facts)

- Vocabulary: Reuse, reduce, recycle, sustainable
- Types of pollution   (air, water, earth, noise)
- Ways that humans can help preserve the environment (reuse, recycle, renew, etc.)

Able to Do (Skills)

- Gather data by reading from the text, various articles, Internet sources, and so on.
- Watch a video on pollution
- Work in discussion groups
- Generate a solution to a pollution problem

Problem: The city of Rubidge has a landfill that is reaching capacity. Environmental scientists predict the landfill will be full in eight years. Determine what living things in the environment might be affected by a full landfill. Generate a solution to the pollution issue that Rubidge community members can participate in.

Lesson Component: Rubric

Environment Rubric

Expectations	Amazing!	Above Average	Average	Additional Effort Needed
Understand ✓ Living things depend upon the environment. ✓ Humans must all work to sustain the planet. 15 Points	❑ Shows complex understanding of the concepts ❑ Supports with data from text ❑ Explores related ideas _____ Points	❑ Understands the concepts ❑ Uses some text references ❑ Explores ideas beyond facts and details _____ Points	❑ Limited understanding of key concepts ❑ Limited text reference ❑ Little depth or elaboration of idea _____ Points	❑ Little understanding of the concept ❑ No or inaccurate reference to text _____ Points
Know ✓ Terms: Reuse, reduce, recycle, sustainable ✓ Types of pollution ✓ Ways to preserve the environment 15 Points	❑ Precise facts ❑ In depth and well supported _____ Points	❑ Covers facts effectively ❑ Well developed _____ Points	❑ Valid facts but little depth or elaboration _____ Points	❑ Needs more facts ❑ Needs accurate facts _____ Points
Quality Work *(as defined below by your group)* 10 Points	❑ Met quality work criteria ❑ Unique, fresh, or imaginative work _____ Points	❑ Met quality work criteria ❑ Creatively integrates work _____ Points	❑ Met quality work criteria _____ Points	❑ Does not meet quality work criteria _____ Points
Group Work/ Notes 10 Points	❑ Encourages others ❑ Collaborates and resolves conflicts _____ Points	❑ Listens well ❑ Helps others ❑ Shares _____ Points	❑ Appropriate effort ❑ Cooperative _____ Points	❑ Inappropriate effort ❑ Not cooperative _____ Points

Type of project: _____skit_____
Ways I/we will do quality work for the project:
1. We will write a script that is creative
2. We will rehearse at least 3 times
3. We will explain our understanding with depth and detail
Teacher Initials: _KK_

What I/we did that was quality work

What I/we would do better next time

Student Grade: _____   Teacher Grade: _____

Comments:

G.5 Environmental Lesson—Contracts

Lesson Component: Student Handout

Pollution and the Environment Contract

I, _____, will demonstrate my understanding of the learning objectives by _____ date.

❑ I understand that this means I will remain focused on my work, and I will study on my own time as well as during school time.

❑ I will be resourceful in finding answers and getting help. I will go to the teacher only as a last resort.

❑ I understand that I must be responsible for my own education and that, if I don't work at learning the science objectives, I may not benefit from my education.

❑ I understand that my grade will be made of three parts: (1) my effort, (2) one task from the contract selected by me, and (3) one task from the contract randomly selected by my teacher.

Contract Part A: Must Do

Read pages 214–229 in your science text. Respond to the questions from the text listed on the board.
Create a graphic organizer that effectively communicates your understanding of the learning objectives for this unit.

Contract Part B: Pick any three activities from the list below

1. Reflect on your connection to the earth and environment. Using a medium of your choice, document your thoughts, what you observe, how you feel, and what you learn about the environment around you.

2. Create a children's book to teach children about pollution and about caring for our environment.

3. Create a game for others to play to learn about pollution and the environment.

4. Use charts and graphs to present data on pollution. Share your data and conclusions in a written or oral presentation.

5. Create a skit or video that is a public service announcement about pollution.

6. Create a news report about the current state of pollution in a location of your choice.

7. Write a piece of poetry or music about how pollution has affected you, your life, or other living things around you.

8. Design a lab that demonstrates how pollution affects the environment.

9. Research ways our school may be creating pollution. Determine what living things in the environment might be affected by our school's pollution. Generate a solution to the pollution issue that students can participate in.

10. Research ways your community may be creating pollution. Determine what living things in the environment might be affected by your community's pollution. Generate a solution to the pollution issue that citizens can participate in.

11. Investigate governmental initiatives you consider to be helping or hindering in controlling the amount and types of pollutants. Give a report to help us understand the connections that you see.

Lesson Component: Rubric

Expectations	Amazing!	Above Average	Average	Additional Effort Needed
Understand ✓ Living things depend upon the environment. ✓ Humans must all work to sustain the planet. 15 Points	❑ Shows complex understanding of the concepts ❑ Supports with data from text ❑ Explores related ideas _____ Points	❑ Understands the concepts ❑ Uses some text references ❑ Explores ideas beyond facts and details _____ Points	❑ Limited understanding of key concepts ❑ Limited text reference ❑ Little depth or elaboration of idea _____ Points	❑ Little understanding of the concept ❑ No or inaccurate reference to text _____ Points
Know ✓ Terms: Reuse, reduce, recycle, sustainable ✓ Types of pollution ✓ Ways to preserve the environment 15 Points	❑ Precise facts ❑ In depth and well supported _____ Points	❑ Covers facts effectively ❑ Well developed _____ Points	❑ Valid facts but little depth or elaboration _____ Points	❑ Needs more facts ❑ Needs accurate facts _____ Points
Quality Work 10 Points	❑ Unique, fresh, or imaginative work _____ Points	❑ Creatively integrates work _____ Points	❑ Met objectives with minimal quality _____ Points	❑ Did not do quality work _____ Points
Work Habits Completion of Contract 10 Points	❑ Highly resourceful ❑ Quality effort ❑ Completed contract beyond expectations _____ Points	❑ Resourceful ❑ Good effort ❑ Completed contract successfully _____ Points	❑ Minimally resourceful ❑ Minimal effort ❑ Met minimal expectations of contract _____ Points	❑ Not resourceful ❑ Little or no effort ❑ Contract incomplete _____ Points
What I did that was quality work				
What I would do better next time				

Student Grade: _____   Teacher Grade: _____

Comments:

G.6 Environmental Lesson—Learning Stations

Component: *Station Planning Guide*

Station Grouping: Students are randomly divided into three groups. Students choose a partner to work with at each of the three stations.		
Station 1: What Is Pollution?		
Objectives Met	Types of pollution Why we must all help	
Materials Needed	• Video: Types of pollution • Note-taking guide • Pencil	• Poster board • Types of paper • Crayons/Markers • Others (as needed)
Structured or Exploratory Activity	Both. Students create a mnemonic with their partners to remember the types of pollution. They complete their own "quick write" to show understanding. Assessment: Students present their mnemonic and turn in their "quick write."	
Station 2: Use It Again, Sam!		
Objectives Met	Know ways to reuse, reduce, and recycle products	
Materials Needed	Chart paper and pencils	Box with milk carton, tin can, single socks, egg cartons, old clothes, gadgets, jar of food scraps—any garbage you have around!
Structured or Exploratory Activity	Exploratory: Students work with partner and select three items from the box. The objective is to make a list or chart of as many ways as possible to reuse, reduce, and recycle the objects. Assessment: Students' charts will be displayed, and I will check those on the rubric.	

Station 3: Recycling Paper		
Objectives Met	We must all care for our planet and learn ways to reduce and reuse products.	
Materials Needed	• Old newspaper • Electric blender • Large pan • Wire screening • Article: "Paper Recycling: Promise or Propaganda?"	• Water • Cornstarch • Stirrer • Wax paper • Rolling pin
Structured or Exploratory Activity	Structured. Students will create recycled paper a few days in advance. They will respond to questions about the paper. They will read an article that presents different points of view about recycling. They will discuss and respond to questions. Assessment: I will randomly select three of their questions to check using the rubric.	

Component: Student Handouts

Station 1: What Is Pollution?
(Objective: Types of Pollution)

1. Watch the video *Types of Pollution*.

2. Using a multiple intelligence strength, work with your partner to create a mnemonic that will help someone with your MI strength remember the different types of pollution.

   a. Music Smart? Create a song, rap, or poem.

   b. Art Smart? Draw a poster, or graphically represent the terms.

   c. Body Smart? *Be* the numbers, and act out the problem, or do some other kind of skit or movement-related activity.

   d. Word Smart? Create an acrostic or word trick.

   e. People Smart? Find a way to get lots of people engaged in learning about the types of pollution.

   f. Self Smart? Create your own, just-for-you, unique way of remembering the types of pollution.

3. Do a "quick write" exit card. What did you learn in this video about how the different types of pollution affect life on the planet?

4. At the end of the class, plan to share what you have created.

Station 2: Use It Again, Sam!
(Objective: Know ways to reuse, reduce, and recycle)

1. With your partner, select three items from the box

2. Brainstorm a list of all the ways you can think of to reuse, reduce, and recycle your item. (You can use the computer to help you search for ideas.)

3. Make a chart that includes each of your items. Display the ways you came up with to reuse, reduce, and recycle them. Remember to do quality work on your chart. Display your chart on the "Use It Again, Sam!" bulletin board.

Station 3: Recycle Paper

After creating your recycled paper, discuss the following questions with your partner. Use the recycled paper to record your thoughts!

Paper Evaluation:

1. Do you feel that the effort to recycle paper is worth the trouble? Why or why not?

2. How many times can paper be recycled?

3. Do you think recycling could create more jobs? Describe the types of jobs it would generate.

Read the article, "Paper Recycling: Promise or Propaganda?" Respond to the following questions.

1. In your opinion, do you think this article supports or discourages recycling?

2. If you think paper recycling is a viable way to preserve the environment, what are some ways you could convince or encourage others to recycle more?

3. If you do <u>not</u> feel paper recycling is a viable way to preserve the environment, what alternatives would you suggest to help preserve the environment?

Directions for Recycling Paper
Paper must be made before doing Center 3.

1. Tear a page of used paper into small pieces. Place the pieces in a large pan. Add enough water to cover the paper, and soak for ten minutes.

2. While the paper is soaking, mix one-fourth of a cup of water with about one-eighth of a cup of cornstarch. Stir until the cornstarch dissolves.

3. Pour off the water in the pan that was not absorbed by the paper.

4. Put the paper in a blender. Add the cornstarch and water mixture. Put the lid on the blender. Run the blender on high for two minutes.

5. Put the screen over the pan. Pour the material onto the screen. With your hands, spread it out so that it is flat and thin. Cover the material with wax paper. Use a rolling pin to squeeze out the excess water. *Carefully* remove the wax paper.

6. Allow the new paper to dry completely. (This may take a day or two.) Gently peel it from the screen. Try writing on it. Write down what happens.

Component: Rubric

Expectations	Amazing!	Above Average	Average	Additional Effort Needed
Center One ➤ Completed quality mnemonic on types of pollution (Know) 10 Points	❑ ___ 8–10	❑ ___ 5–7	❑ ___ 2–4	❑ ___ 0–1
➤ Quick write (Understand) 10 Points	❑ ___ 8–10	❑ ___ 5–7	❑ ___ 2–4	❑ ___ 0–1
Center Two ➤ Completed quality chart of products (Able to Do) 10 Points	❑ ___ 8–10	❑ ___ 5–7	❑ ___ 2–4	❑ ___ 0–1
Center Three ➤ Completed discussion questions. (Understand) 10 Points	❑ ___ 8–10	❑ ___ 5–7	❑ ___ 2–4	❑ ___ 0–1

G.7 Environmental Lesson—Compacting

Lesson Component: *Student Handout*

Congratulations!
You have successfully tested out of the environment unit. You have bought yourself time to work more deeply on a project related to environmental issues. Here are some issues you may want to look into, or you may have something of your own that you would like to research or do. When you have decided what you want to do, check with me, and we will make a plan for your learning.

Global Warming

    Reality or myth?
    Global warming: past, present, and future

Pollution Solutions

    Water as fuel—is it really better for the environment?
    Hydrogen, wind energy, solar resources—why don't we have more of these?

Relationships Between Economy and the Environment

    Can money be made taking care of the environment?
    Does the economy affect the environment?

Investigating the Effects

    Conduct experimental research, and collect empirical data—see me for resources

Lesson Component: *Rubric*

Expectations	Amazing!	Above Average	Average	Additional Effort Needed
Understand ✓ Living things depend upon the environment. ✓ Humans must all work to sustain the planet. 15 Points	❏ Shows complex understanding of the concepts ❏ Supports with data from text ❏ Explores related ideas _____ Points	❏ Understands the concepts ❏ Uses some text references ❏ Explores ideas beyond facts and details _____ Points	❏ Limited understanding of key concepts ❏ Limited text reference ❏ Little depth or elaboration of idea _____ Points	❏ Little understanding of the concept ❏ No or inaccurate reference to text _____ Points
Know ✓ Terms: Reuse, reduce, recycle, sustainable ✓ Types of pollution ✓ Ways to preserve the environment 15 Points	❏ Precise facts ❏ In depth and well supported _____ Points	❏ Covers facts effectively ❏ Well developed _____ Points	❏ Valid facts but little depth or elaboration _____ Points	❏ Needs more facts ❏ Needs accurate facts _____ Points
Quality Work 10 Points	❏ Unique, fresh, or imaginative work _____ Points	❏ Creatively integrates work _____ Points	❏ Met objectives with minimal quality _____ Points	❏ Did not do quality work _____ Points
Work Habits Completion of Contract 10 Points	❏ Highly resourceful ❏ Quality effort ❏ Completed contract beyond expectations _____ Points	❏ Resourceful ❏ Good effort ❏ Completed contract successfully _____ Points	❏ Minimally resourceful ❏ Minimal effort ❏ Met minimal expectations of contract _____ Points	❏ Not resourceful ❏ Little or no effort ❏ Contract incomplete _____ Points

What I did that was quality work
What I would do better next time

Student Grade: _____   Teacher Grade: _____

Comments:

H.1 Lesson Template: Tic-Tac-Toe

1.	2.	3.
4.	5.	6.
7.	8.	9.

Directions: Choose activities in a tic-tac-toe design. When you have completed the activities in a row—horizontally, vertically, or diagonally—you may decide to be finished. Or you may decide to keep going and complete more activities.

I choose activities # _____, # _____, # _____, # _____

Do you have ideas for alternate activities you'd like to do instead? Talk them over with your teacher.

I prefer to do the following alternate activities: _____

_____

Name: _____

Date Received:_____ Date Due:_____

Date Completed:_____

H.2 Lesson Template: Cubing

Understand:

Know:

Able to Do:

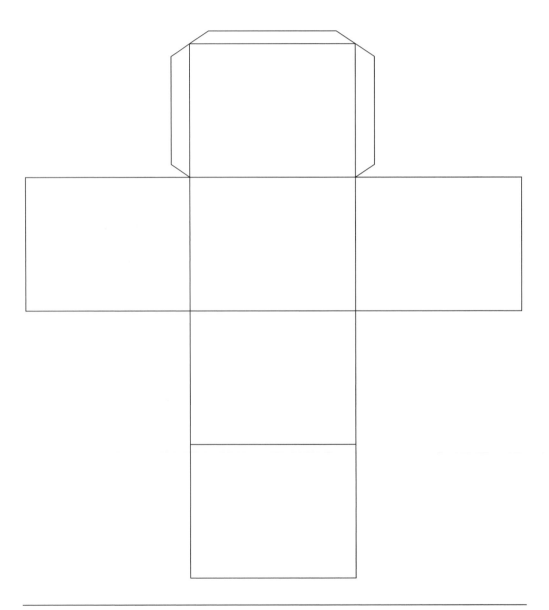

H.3 Lesson Template: Destination Dice

Destination Dice!

You will be working in groups of three to complete six activities that will help you gain a deeper understanding of our learning target.

Understand:

Know:

Able to Do:

Now You Get It:

The "Destination Dice" handout you received is unique for your group's readiness level. Each card on the handout corresponds to the numbers on a die. Take turns rolling the die to determine your destiny. The activities that correspond with the numbers you roll will be the activities you are responsible for (two each). Roll until all six activities are assigned. Work on your assigned cards, asking for guidance from your teammates when necessary. Once all six cards are complete, take turns reflecting on these activities, where they brought you in your understanding, and checking with your partners to see that they understand all activities too. No one understands until we all understand!

Dicing Sheet Template

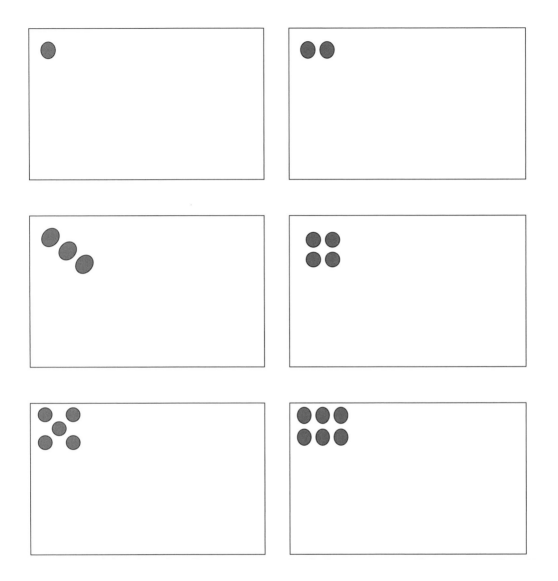

H.4 Lesson Template: RAFT Plus

Understand:

Know:

Able to Do:

Role:
Audience:
Format:
Task (Activity):

I.1 Planning Guide: Designing a Student Contract

_____ Use the learning target to develop outcomes. Ask yourself . . .
- ❑ Does each choice align with the *Understand, Know,* and *Able to do* components?
- ❑ Are these activities expanding upon the core activities that all students must complete?
- ❑ Is there a balance of outcomes for various learning styles?
- ❑ How will each task be weighted?

_____ Create a list of conditions the students agree to accept in the contract. Ask yourself . . .
- ❑ Am I holding them accountable if they do not fulfill their obligations?
- ❑ Are the working habits and skills needed to complete the contract made clear?

_____ Develop a plan of action with the students for each day's work session. Ask yourself . . .
- ❑ Does the student have all necessary materials?
- ❑ Have arrangements been made for the student to work in other areas of the school?

_____ Students and the teacher must sign the contract. You may also decide to have parents sign the contract.

_____ Determine how you will assess the student throughout the process and how you will assess yourself and the contract design at the end. Ask yourself . . .
- ❑ What worked? What didn't work?
- ❑ What management strategies need to change?
- ❑ What further planning do I need to do to improve the next contract?

I.2 Example: Student Work Contract

Student Name:_____

Having tested out of a unit, I promise to do the following:

1. I will select and complete an alternative assignment.

2. I will use my time wisely, and, using my "Goal Setting Log," I will keep track of the work I complete each day.

3. If I need help, I will wait until the teacher is not busy.

4. If no one can help, I will try to keep working or move to another activity.

5. I will not bother other students or the teacher.

6. I will not brag about working on an alternative assignment to other students.

7. I will complete the projects I choose to do and turn them in to the teacher.

Student Signature: _____

I agree to help the student follow this plan.

Teacher Signature: _____

Date: _____

I.3 Template: Work Log
(for individuals or groups)

Date	Daily Work Plan	Work Actually Completed

I.4 Planning Guide for Learning Stations

Concept:

Understand:

Know:

Able to Do:

Station 1 Title:

Objectives Met:

Materials Needed:

Structured or Exploratory Activity:

Accountability:

Will students be

- o keeping a daily work log?
- o completing exit cards at each station?
- o doing a "partner progress" check?
- o turning in work along the way?
- o self-reflecting on progress (scale of 1–5; how to make improvements)?

Other?

Station 2 Title:

Objectives Met:

Materials Needed:

Structured or Exploratory Activity:

Station 3 Title:

Objectives Met:

Materials Needed:

Structured or Exploratory Activity:

I.5 Planning Guide: Curriculum Compacting

1. Subject Area Being Studied: _____

2. Pretesting Method:

3. Options for Alternative Work:
   _____ a. Activity Extension Menu
   _____ b. Independent Project
   _____ c. Other

4. Expectations for Regular Unit Instruction
   _____ a. Unit quizzes and/or final
   _____ b. Unit special events
   _____ c. Subject matter not passed on pretest

5. Record Keeping
   _____ a. Compacting Contract
   _____ b. Daily Work Log
   _____ c. Daily Exit Cards
   _____ d. Evaluation Contract

J.1 Quality Work Self-Assessment

Name _____   Unit _____   Date _____

Quality Skill	Super	Standard	So-So	Slipped
Listening to discussions and directions				
Understanding key concepts				
Taking complete and organized notes				
Completing warm-ups				
Asking questions when need to know more				
Being responsible during lab work				
Completing homework				
Studying for tests				

Put a star next to the categories above in which you feel you did quality work.

Below, list the categories in which you need to improve your quality of work.

Are you willing to improve your quality of work in any of these areas? If so, which areas and what will you do to improve?

Area:_____   Improvement:_____

Area:_____   Improvement:_____

Created by **Kathleen Kryza**

J.2 Exit Card Template

STATION EXIT CARD: Self-Assessment					
Name		**Station**			
	Low				High
I used my station time wisely.	**1**	**2**	**3**	**4**	**5**
I completed the station task.	**1**	**2**	**3**	**4**	**5**
I understood the objectives of the station.	**1**	**2**	**3**	**4**	**5**

What I learned:

Some questions I have:

J.3 Quality Work Criteria

Following are some ideas to help students define quality work, and these criteria can be used in rubrics.

Quality Writing Project

➤ High level content
➤ Meaningful details
➤ Neat/Organized/Typed
➤ Writing conventions followed

Quality (Skit/Play)

➤ Memorize script
➤ Costumes/Props
➤ Well acted
➤ Can be heard clearly

Quality (Poster/Visual)

➤ Vivid colors
➤ Flow
➤ Easy to read
➤ Unique and clear message

Quality (Song)
➤ Original
➤ Taped/Live/Video
➤ Costumes/Instruments
➤ Loud and clear voice

Quality (Children's Book)
➤ Colorful, well-drawn pictures
➤ Language and content appropriate for age group
➤ Cover page attractive
➤ Writing conventions followed

Group Work (high to low)

➤ Encourages others; collaborates and resolves conflicts
➤ Listens well; helps others; shares
➤ Appropriate effort; cooperative
➤ Inappropriate effort; not cooperative

Work Habits

➤ Uses time well; self-motivated; effort beyond average
➤ Time on task; appropriate effort
➤ Little time on task or effort
➤ Not working; resistant

Presentation

➤ Dynamic and compelling
➤ Interest holding
➤ Not so interesting
➤ Sleep inducing

Effort and Preparation

➤ Considerable
➤ More than average
➤ Sufficient
➤ Minimal or none

Visual Aids

➤ Extensive; attractive; enhance information
➤ Appropriate number and quality; work with information
➤ Few in number and quality; little value
➤ Minimal or none

J.4 C U KAN Rubric Template

Expectations	Amazing	Above Average	Average	Awful
Understand _____ Points	❏ Shows complex understanding of the concepts ❏ Supports with data from text ❏ Explores related ideas _____ Points	❏ Understands the concepts ❏ Uses some text references ❏ Explores ideas beyond facts and details _____ Points	❏ Limited understanding of key concepts ❏ Limited text reference ❏ Little depth or elaboration of idea _____ Points	❏ Little understanding of the concept ❏ No or inaccurate reference to text _____ Points
Know _____ Points	❏ Precise facts ❏ In depth and well supported _____ Points	❏ Covers facts effectively ❏ Well developed _____ Points	❏ Valid facts but little depth or elaboration _____ Points	❏ Needs more facts ❏ Needs accurate facts _____ Points
Quality Work _(as defined by your group. See below)_ _____ Points	❏ Met quality work criteria ❏ Unique, fresh, or imaginative work _____ Points	❏ Met quality work criteria ❏ Creatively integrates work _____ Points	❏ Met quality work criteria _____ Points	❏ Does not meet quality work criteria _____ Points
_____ Points	_____ Points	_____ Points	_____ Points	_____ Points

What I/we did that was quality work:

What I/we can improve upon next time:

Ways I/we will do quality work for the project:

1. _____

2. _____

3. _____

Student Grade: _____   Teacher Grade: _____

Comments:

J.5 Rubric Template

SCALE (Use Numbers, Words, Pictures)

Expectations				
Understand _____ Points				
Know _____ Points				
Quality Work _(as defined by student)_ _____ Points				
Work Habits/ Group Work _____ Points				

What I/we did that was quality work:

What I/we can improve upon next time:

Ways I/we will do quality work for the project:

1. _____

2. _____

3. _____

Student Grade: _____   Teacher Grade: _____

Comments:

K.1 Further Readings

Chapman, C., & Freeman, L. (1996). *Multiple intelligences centers and projects.* Thousand Oaks, CA: Corwin Press.

Cohen, E. G. (1994). *Designing groupwork: Strategies for the heterogeneous classroom* (2nd ed.). New York: Teachers College Press.

Erickson, H. L. (2000). *Stirring the head, heart and soul: Redefining curriculum and instruction* (2nd ed.). Thousand Oaks, CA: Corwin Press.

Glasser, W. (1993). *The quality school teacher.* New York: HarperCollins.

Gregory, G., & Chapman, C. (2002). *Differentiated instructional strategies: One size doesn't fit all.* Thousand Oaks, CA: Corwin Press.

Jensen, E. (2000). *Different brains, different learners: How to reach the hard to reach.* Thousand Oaks, CA: Corwin Press.

Jensen, E. (1998). *Teaching with the brain in mind.* Alexandria, VA: Association for Supervision and Curriculum Development.

Kingore, B. (2002). *Rubrics and more!* Austin, TX: Professional Associates.

Kottler, E., & Kottler, J. A. (2002). *Children with limited English: Teaching strategies for the regular classroom.* Thousand Oaks, CA: Corwin Press.

Silver, H., Strong, R., & Perini, M. (2000). *So each may learn: Integrating learning styles and multiple intelligences.* Alexandria, VA: Association for Supervision and Curriculum Development.

Tomlinson, C. A. (2001). *How to differentiate instruction in mixed-ability classrooms* (2nd ed.). Alexandria, VA: Association for Supervision and Curriculum Development.

Tomlinson, C. A. (2004). *Fulfilling the promise of the differentiated classroom: Strategies and tools for responsive teaching.* Alexandria, VA: Association for Supervision and Curriculum Development.

Weinbrenner, S. (1996). *Teaching kids with learning difficulties in the regular classroom.* Minneapolis: Free Spirit.

Weinbrenner, S. (2001). *Teaching gifted kids in the regular classroom.* Minneapolis: Free Spirit.

Wolfe, P. (2001). *Brain matters: Translating research into classroom practice.* Alexandria, VA: Association for Supervision and Curriculum Development.

K.2 Varied Level Texts

Lerner Classroom
www.lernerclassroom.com
Leveled nonfiction books & teaching guides
Social Studies, Science, Reading/Literacy
K–8

Redbrick
www.redbricklearning.com
Leveled nonfiction for grades
K–8

National Geographic
www.nationalgeographic.com/education
Nonfiction & content-based fiction
Reading Comprehension, Expository Writing, Differentiated Theme Sets
K–12

Time for Kids
www.teachercreated.com
Nonfiction & fiction in the content areas
K–12

Pearson AGS Globe
www.agsglobe.com
Middle and high school high-interest and varied reading level text resources
6–12

Bibliography

Asher, J. (2000). *Learning another language through actions*. Los Gatos, CA: Sky Oaks Productions.

Association of Graduate Careers Advisory Services. (2005). First impressions. In *The interview itself*. Retrieved May 6, 2006, from http://www.prospects .ac.uk/cms/ShowPage/Home_page/Applications_and_interviews/Int erviews/The_interview_itself/p!elpgeg

Biancarosa, C., & Snow, C. E. (2006). *Reading next—A vision for action and research in middle and high school literacy: A report to Carnegie Corporation of New York* (2nd ed.).Washington, DC: Alliance for Excellent Education.

Collins, A., Brown, J. S., & Newman, S. E. (1989). Cognitive apprenticeship: Teaching the craft of reading, writing, and mathematics. In L. B. Resnick (Ed.), *Knowing, learning, and instruction: Essays in honor of Robert Glaser* (pp. 453–494). Hillsdale, NJ: Lawrence Erlbaum.

Jensen, E. (1998). *Teaching with the brain in mind.* Alexandria, VA: Association for Supervision and Curriculum Development.

Klem, A. M., & Connell, J. P. (2004). Relationships matter: Linking teacher support to student engagement and achievement. *Journal of School Health, 74*(7), 262–273.

Pearson, P. D., & Gallagher, M. (1983). The instruction of reading comprehension. *Contemporary Educational Psychology, 8*, 317–344.

Secretan, L. (2004). *Inspire: What great leaders do.* Hoboken, NJ: John Wiley.

Secretan, L. (2006). *One: The art and practice of conscious leadership.* Ontario, Canada: The Secretan Center.

Sousa, D. (2006). *How the brain learns* (Third Ed.). Thousand Oaks, CA: Corwin Press.

Tomlinson, C. A. (1999). *The differentiated classroom: Responding to the needs of all learners.* Alexandria, VA: Association for Supervision and Curriculum Development.

Tomlinson, C. A., & McTighe, J. (2006). *Integrating differentiated instruction + understanding by design.* Alexandria, VA: Association for Supervision and Curriculum Development.

Vygotsky, L. (1978). *Mind in society: The development of higher psychological processes.* Cambridge, MA: Harvard University Press.

Wiggins, G., & McTighe, J. (1998). *Understanding by design.* Alexandria, VA: Association for Supervision and Curriculum Development.

Index

"Able to do" objective, overview, 66 (fig), 69 (fig)

Academic scores, 21 (fig)

Adding fractions mnemonic, 59

Advanced learner
  anchor activity for, 45–46
  multifaceted investigation for, 45–46

Affirmation poster, 26

Analytical thinker. *See* Sternberg processing preferences

Anchor activity
  advanced learner, 45–46
  individual inquiry, 201
  language arts, 200
  mathematics, 200
  miscellaneous, 201
  music/art, 201
  physical education, 201
  science, 200
  social studies, 200

Anticipation guide, vocabulary, 56

Apprenticeship. *See* Lifelong learning, apprenticeship approach to

Assessment
  exit card (*See* Exit card)
  meaningful, 68
  pre-assessment, 76, 119, 169
  quality work criteria, 70, 241
  self-assessment, 68, 73, 76, 77, 239
  vs. grading, 169
  See also Assessment, ongoing; Assessment tips; C U Kan

Assessment, ongoing
  after learning, 170, 173 (fig)
  before learning, 169–170, 171 (fig)
  during learning, 170, 172 (fig)
  vignette about, 167–169

Assessment, *vs.* grading, 169

Assessment tips, 76–77
  choice menus, 91
  compacting, 164
  contracts, 131
  learning stations, 148–149
  RAFT Plus, 101
  tiered lessons, 119

Balanced grading system, 174 (fig)–175

Ball toss, 57

Bingo, vocabulary, 55–56

Brain research, 6–7, 14 (fig)

Brainstorming, 10, 20, 51, 168

C U KAN
  "Able to do" objective, 66 (fig), 69 (fig)
  assessment tips, 76
  assessment tips, for group, 76–77
  clear learning target example, 70 (fig)
  components of, 65–66 (fig)
  "Concept" objective, 66 (fig), 69 (fig)
  deep/dynamic lesson designs for, 77–78 (fig)
  differentiating instruction and, 77
  environmental lesson design, 207
  "Know" objective, 66 (fig), 69 (fig)
  learning target sample, 69 (fig)
  learning target template, 205
  management level tips, 75
  meaningful assessment and, 68
  meaningful instruction and, 67–68
  meaningful learning and, 67
  "Now you get it" objective, 66 (fig), 69 (fig)
  planning guide template, 206
  reasons to use, 67–68

rubric example, 74 (fig)
rubric template, 242
teacher self-assessment, 76
teaching tips, for all lesson
    designs, 73, 75–77
"Understand" objective, 66 (fig),
    69 (fig)
writing, 68, 69 (fig)
See also C U KAN sample; Choice
    menus; Compacting; Contracts;
    Learning stations; RAFT Plus;
    Tiered lessons
C U KAN sample, 68, 70–73
"Able to do" objective, 73
"Know" objective, 70
learning target example, 70 (fig),
    72 (fig)
"Now you get it" objective, 73
planning guide example, 71 (fig)
"Quality Work" objective, 70
rubric, 68, 70–73
rubric, using with student, 73
student handout example, 72 (fig)
"Understand" objective, 70
Challenge. *See* Compacting
Charades, vocabulary, 56
Check, 16 (fig), 17, 44 (fig), 202
according to learning profile,
    46–50, 54–57, 61–62
according to readiness, 46, 47 (fig)
C U KAN and, 77
pre-assessment and, 169
varying text levels, 61–62
vocabulary instruction, 54–57
Chew, 16 (fig), 17, 44 (fig), 202
C U KAN and, 77
graphic organizers and, 63
pre-assessment and, 169
Choice, according to learning
    style, 46–50
for vocabulary, 48–50
on homework, 47–48
tests, student choices on, 48
Choice menus
assessment tips, 91
environmental lesson example, 208
language arts example, 89
lesson design tips, 90
management tips, 90
mathematics example, 82–83
mathematics example, rubric, 83
science example, 84–85
social studies example, 86–88

social studies example, rubric, 87–88
subject content examples, 82–89
teacher overview, 80–81
teacher self-assessment, 91
teaching tips, 90–91
Choice theory, 14 (fig)
Chunk, 16 (fig), 17, 44 (fig), 202
according to learning profile,
    50–53 (fig), 61–64
C U KAN and, 77
graphic organizers, 50–53 (fig), 63
memory techniques, 62–64
pre-assessment and, 169
varying text levels, 61–62
Chunk, Chew, and *Check* framework,
    16 (fig), 17, 202–203
See also *Check*; *Chew*; *Chunk*
Cluster maps, 52
Collaboration, 10
Commitment. *See* Contracts
Community, based on honoring
    diversity, 5, 7, 13, 14 (fig), 26–30
traditional classroom and, 6
using student data for, 26–28
Compacting
assessment tips, 164
content subject examples, 152–163
environmental lesson, 227
environmental lesson rubric, 228
language arts, 161–163
lesson design tips, 164
management tips, 164
mathematics example, 152–154
mathematics example, rubric,
    153–154
planning guide, 238
science example, 155–157
science example, rubric, 157
social studies example, 158–160
teacher overview, 150–151
teacher self-assessment, 164
teaching tips, 164
"Concept" objective, overview,
    66 (fig), 69 (fig)
Constructivism, 14 (fig)
Content, 16 (fig), 17
Content subject examples
choice menus, 82–89
compacting, 152–163
contracts, 122–129
learning stations, 134–147
RAFT Plus, 94–100
tiered lessons, 104–117

Contracts
  assessment tips, 131
  content subject examples, 122–129
  designing, 234
  environmental lesson, 218–219
  environmental lesson, rubric, 220
  example, 235
  language arts example, 128–129
  lesson design tips, 130
  management tips, 130
  mathematics example, 122–123
  planning guide, 234–235
  science example, 124–125
  social studies example, 126–127
  teacher overview, 120–121
  teacher self-assessment, 131
  teaching tips, 130–131
Copy change, 63
Creation question, 47 (fig)
Creative thinker. *See* Sternberg
    processing preferences
Cubing lesson template, 230
Curriculum compacting planning
    guide, 238

Deep and dynamic lesson design, 77–79
  benefits of, 78 (fig)
  See also Choice menus; Compacting;
    Contracts; Learning stations;
    Lite-n-lean strategy; RAFT
    Plus; Tiered lessons
Describe/retell question, 47 (fig)
Destination Dice, 104–107
  lesson template, 231–232
Differential teaching, *vs.* traditional
    teaching, 32 (fig)–33
Differentiating classroom instruction,
    16–18, 44 (fig)
  See also *Check*; *Chew*; *Chunk*;
    Content; Environment
Discussion/journaling questions,
    46, 47 (fig)
Diversity. *See* Community, based
    on honoring diversity

English language arts. *See* Language
    arts
Environment, classroom, 16 (fig),
    17, 44 (fig)
  affirmation posters for, 26
  community/diversity in, 28–30
  emotional tone of, 25–26, 29
  modeling honor/inspiration in, 26

physical setting, 25, 28
  routines, 25
  routines, group, 28–29
Environmental lesson
  C U Kan for, 207
  choice design, 208
  choice menu, 209
  compacting, 227
  compacting, rubric, 228
  contracts, 218–219
  contracts, rubric, 220
  learning stations, 221–225
  learning stations, rubric, 226
  lesson component rubric, 213
  RAFT Plus, 211–212
  rubric for, 210
  tiered lessons, 214–216
  tiered lessons, rubric, 217
Exit card
  compacted assignment, 164
  contracts, 131
  for pre-assessment, 119
  language arts, 146, 147, 148
  mathematics, 134, 136–137
  quick write, 167–168
  template for, 240
Fact question, 47 (fig)
Fulghum, Robert, 26
Further readings, 244
  varied level texts, 245

General interest inventory, 192
Geography interest-based project, 60
Grading, 170, 172–175
  balanced grading system,
    174 (fig)–175
  criteria for, 173–174
  vs. assessment, 169
Graphic organizer, 50–53 (fig)
  computerized, 52
  for note-taking, 63–64 (fig)
  for vocabulary, 53 (fig)
Group
  discussion/journaling questions
    for, 46
  graphic organizers and, 51–52
Group behavior chart, 198
Group classroom routines, 28
  anchor activities, 29
  core groups, 28
  transitioning in/out of groups, 28
Group contract sample, 195–196
Group processing sheet sample, 197

Health/physical education
    interest-based project, 61
History interest-based project, 60
Homework, student choices on, 47–48

Independent investigation, for
    advanced learner, 45–46
Individual inquiry, anchor activities
    for, 201
Information, 16 (fig), 44 (fig)
Information readiness
    according to student interests,
        57–59
    interest-based projects, 60–61
    investigations for advanced
        learners, 45–46
    See also Tiered lessons
Input. See Chunk
Inspiration, vs. motivation, 4–5
Inspiration (computer graphic
    organizer), 52
Inspiring classroom
    defining, 11
    foundations of, 5–7, 182
    goal setting for, 183
    key learning theories and,
        13–14 (fig)
    vs. traditional classroom, 5–6
Instructional practices, elements
        to differentiate, 15–18
    Chunk, Chew, and Check framework
        for, 16 (fig), 17
    content, 16 (fig), 17
    environment, 16 (fig), 17
    overview of, 16 (fig), 18 (fig),
        44 (fig)
Instructional practices, routine
    teaching, 15
Interactive note taking, 63–64
Interest inventory, 21 (fig), 192, 193
Interest-based projects, 60–61
Internet resources, 10

Journaling/discussion questions,
    46, 47 (fig)
Judge question, 47 (fig)

Kiddie vocabulary, 55
Kidspiration (computer graphic
    organizer), 52
"Know" objective, overview,
    66 (fig), 69 (fig)
KWL, 50, 51

Language arts
    anchor activities for, 200
    learning targets sample, 69 (fig)
    See also Language arts example
Language arts example
    choice menus, 89
    compacting, 161–163
    contracts, 128–129
    learning stations, 145–147
    RAFT Plus, 99–100
    tiered lessons, 115–117
Language arts/English interest-based
        project, 60
Learner profile card, 24
Learners, honoring/inspiring,
        7, 10–11, 13, 14 (fig)
    gathering student data for, 20–23
    traditional classroom and, 5, 6
Learning preferences, 21 (fig)
Learning preferences questionnaire, 194
Learning profile project, 57–59
    adding fractions mnemonics, 59
    scientific methods mnemonics, 58
    varying text levels, 61–62
Learning profiles
    varying (See Learning stations)
    vocabulary and, 54–57
Learning specialist, collaboration
    with, 10
Learning stations
    assessment tips, 148–149
    content subject examples, 134–147
    environmental lesson example,
        221–225
    environmental lesson example,
        rubric, 226
    language arts example, 145–147
    lesson design tips, 148
    management tips, 148
    mathematics example, 134–137
    planning guide for, 237
    science example, 137–142
    social studies example, 143–144
    teacher overview, 132–133
    teacher self-assessment, 149
    teaching tips, 148–149
    vocabulary, 56
Learning styles, 21 (fig)
    grouping for different purposes,
        27 (fig)–28
    key for, 55
    survey for, 21–22 (fig)
    See also Choice

Learning styles inventory, 190–191

Lerner Classroom, 245

Lesson, engaging/meaningful, 5, 7, 13, 14 (fig)
    traditional classroom and, 6

Lesson design. *See* Deep and dynamic lesson design; Lite-n-lean strategy

Lesson template
    cubing, 230
    Destination Dice, 231–232
    RAFT Plus, 233
    Tic-Tac-Toe, 229

Lifelong learning, apprenticeship approach to
    shift from traditional to differentiated interactions, 33 (fig)–34
    traditional/differentiated teaching for, 32 (fig)–33
    vital know-hows for, 33 (fig)–36
    vital know-hows for, how to teach, 36–40

Lite-n-lean strategy
    for vocabulary instruction, 54–57
    graphic organizers, 50–53 (fig)
    investigations for advanced learners, 45–46
    learning profile projects, 57–61
    memory techniques, 62–64
    offering students choices, 46–50
    questions for discussion/ journaling, 46, 47 (fig)
    varying text levels, 61–62
    See also Deep and dynamic lesson design

Literary circles, 60

Management tips
    choice menus, 90
    compacting, 164
    contracts, 130
    learning stations, 148
    RAFT Plus, 101
    tiered lessons, 118–119

Matching cards, vocabulary, 56, 57

Mathematics
    adding fractions mnemonic, 59
    anchor activities for, 200
    interest-based project, 60, 61
    learning targets sample, 69 (fig)
    See also Mathematics example

Mathematics example
    choice menus, 47–48, 82–83
    compacting, 152–154
    contracts, 122–123
    learning stations, 134–137
    RAFT Plus, 94–95
    tiered lessons, 104–107

McTighe, Jay, 65, 174

Memory techniques, 62–64
    copy change, 63
    interactive note taking, 63–64
    Total Physical Response, 63

Metacognition, 34

Middle school/high school anchor activities, 200–201

Mind map, 51

Motivation, *vs.* inspiration, 4–5

Multiple intelligences, 27

Multiple intelligences survey, 184–185
    rubric for, 186

Music/art, anchor activities for, 201

National Geographic, 245

Note taking, interactive, 63–64

"Now you get it" objective, overview, 66 (fig), 69 (fig)

One-page list, 21–22

One-size-fits-all teaching, 14, 20, 177

Output. *See* Check

Outside expert, collaboration with, 10

Parents, collaboration with, 10

Pearson AFS Globe, 245

Perspective. *See* RAFT Plus

Physical education, anchor activities for, 201

Picture words, 55

Planning guide
    C U KAN example, 71 (fig)
    C U KAN template, 206
    compacting, 238
    contract, 234–235
    learning stations, 237

Practical thinker. *See* Sternberg processing preferences

Pre-assessment, 76, 119, 169

Pre-assessment exit card, 119

Process. *See* Chew

Quality work criteria, 70, 241

Quality work self-assessment, 239

Questions, discussion/journaling, 46, 47 (fig)
Quick write exit card, 167–168

RAFT Plus
    assessment tips, 101
    content subject example, 94–100
    environmental lesson example, 211–212
    language arts example, 99–100
    language arts example, rubric, 100
    lesson design tips, 101
    lesson template, 233
    management tips, 101
    mathematics example, 94–95
    mathematics example, rubric, 95
    science example, 96
    social studies example, 97–98, 113–114
    social studies example, rubric, 98
    teacher overview, 92–93
    teacher self-assessment, 101
    teaching tips, 101
Readiness
    interest-based projects, 60–61
    investigations for advanced learners, 45–46
    questions for discussions/journaling, 46, 47 (fig)
    See also Tiered lessons
Reading ability
    varying text levels for, 61–62, 245
    See also Language arts
Redbrick, 245
Relevance question, 47 (fig)
Rote memorization, and teaching vocabulary, 54

Same/different question, 47 (fig)
Scaffolding, 33 (fig), 38–39
SCALE rubric template, 243
Science
    anchor activities for, 200
    choice on tests, 48
    interest-based project for, 60
    learning targets sample, 69 (fig)
    See also Science example
Science example
    choice menus, 84–85
    compacting, 155–157
    contracts, 124–125
    learning stations, 137–142
    RAFT Plus, 96
    tiered lessons, 108–112

Scientific method mnemonics, 58
Secretan, Lance, 4
Self-advocacy, student, 24–25
Self-assessment
    group, 77
    quality work, 239
    student, 68, 73, 76
    See also Teacher self-assessment
Self-reflection, student, 68, 77, 170
Self-regulation, student, 38
Skit, quality criteria for, 75
Social studies
    anchor activities for, 200
    learning targets sample, 69 (fig)
    See also social studies example
Social studies example
    choice menus, 86–88
    compacting, 158–160
    contracts, 126–127
    learning stations, 143–144
    RAFT Plus, 97–98
    tiered lessons, 113–114
Specific content inventory, 193
Specific interest inventory
    examples of, 193
Sternberg Processing Preferences, 187–188
    interpretation of, 189
Student apathy, 4–5
Student data, gathering, 20–23
    academic scores, 21 (fig)
    interest inventory, 21 (fig)
    learner profile card, 22, 23 (fig)
    learning preferences, 21 (fig)
    learning preferences survey, 23 (fig)
    learning styles, 21 (fig)
    learning styles survey, 21–22 (fig)
    one page list for, 21–22 (fig)
    tick marks for, 22
    types of data, 21 (fig)
Students, knowing/honoring, 10–11
    gathering data to learn about, 20–23
    using data to build community/honor diversity, 26–28
    using data to honor students, 24–25
Surveys/questionnaires
    data index card, 23 (fig)
    general interest inventory, 192
    learning preference questionnaire, 23 (fig), 194
    learning styles inventory, 21–22 (fig), 190–191

multiple intelligences survey/
    rubric, 184–186
specific content inventory, 193
specific interest inventory, 193
See also Exit card
Sternberg processing preferences,
    187–189, 190–191

Teacher, inspiring
    assessing own growth, 175–176
    beliefs on student learning, 8–9
    collaboration and, 9–10, 175
    core beliefs of, 8–9
    creating inspiring legacy, 177–178
    inspiration from students, 7–8
    self-reflection, 176
Teacher self-assessment
    choice menus, 91
    compacting, 164
    contracts, 131
    learning stations, 149
    RAFT Plus, 101
    tiered lessons, 119
    Team-building activities, 29
    See also Group
Test
    standardized, 48
    student choices on, 48
Text, varied level, 61–62, 245
Textbook resources, 10
Think alouds, 36–37 (fig), 62
Tic-Tac-Toe lesson template, 229
Tiered lessons
    assessment tips, 119
    content subject examples, 104–117
    environmental lesson example,
        214–216
    environmental lesson example,
        rubric, 217
    language arts example, 115–117
    language arts example, rubric,
        116–117
    lesson design tips, 118
    management tips, 118–119
    mathematics example, 104–107
    science example, 108–112
    science example, rubric, 112
    social studies example, 113–114
    social studies example, rubric, 114
    teacher overview, 102–103

teacher self-assessment, 119
    teaching tips, 118–119
Time for Kids, 245
Tomlinson, Carol Ann, 65, 173–174
Total Physical Response (TPR), 63
Tracking, 6
Traditional classroom, as not
    inspiring, 5–6
Traditional teaching, *vs.* differential
    teaching, 32 (fig)–33

"Understandings" objective
    example/non-example of, 204
    overview of, 66 (fig), 69 (fig)

Varied level texts, 61–62, 245
Vital know-hows (VKHs), 33 (fig)–36
    bibliography for, 199
    collaborative/cooperative learning,
        35–36
    discussion/discourse, 34
    inquiry/research, 35
    read/write for understanding, 34–35
    reflective learning, 34
Vital know-hows (VKHs), how to
    teach, 36–40
    explicit instruction, 37 (fig)
    modeling/think alouds, 36–37 (fig)
    scaffolding, 38–39
Vocabulary
    student choice and, 48–50
    See also Vocabulary instruction,
        and learning profiles
Vocabulary instruction, and
    learning profiles, 54–57
    anticipation guides, 56
    ball toss, 57
    bingo, 55–56
    charades, 56
    kiddie vocabulary, 55
    learning stations, 56
    matching cards, 56
    moving matching cards, 57
    picture words, 55
Vocabulary mapping, 52–53 (fig)

Wiggins, Grant, 65
Work log, 151
    template for, 156, 236
Writing genres, 35, 60

CORWIN PRESS